BACK YARD to BACK PACK

Published in 2019 by Murdoch Books, an imprint of Allen & Unwin

Murdoch Books Australia
83 Alexander Street, Crows Nest NSW 2065
Phone: +61 (0)2 8425 0100
murdochbooks.com.au
info@murdochbooks.com.au

Murdoch Books UK
Ormond House, 26–27 Boswell Street, London WC1N 3JZ
Phone: +44 (0) 20 8785 5995
murdochbooks.co.uk
info@murdochbooks.co.uk

 A catalogue record for this book is available from the National Library of Australia

A catalogue record for this book is available from the British Library

ISBN 978 1 76052 469 2 Australia
ISBN 978 1 91163 229 0 UK

Cover design by Design by Committee
Photography © Evie Farrell
Cover photography © Evie Farrell

Printed and bound in Australia by Griffin Press

 The paper in this book is FSC certified. FSC promotes environmentally responsible, socially beneficial and economically viable management of the world's forests.

Evie Farrell

BACK YARD to BACK PACK

A solo mum, a six year old
and a life-changing adventure

murdoch books

Sydney | London

For my Emmie, who changed my life.
And for George, who inspired me to live it.

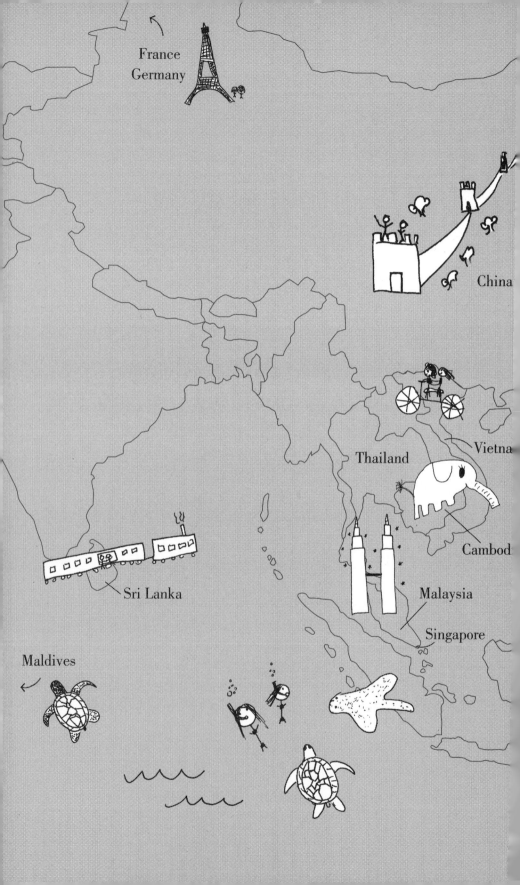

France
Germany

China

Vietna

Thailand

Cambod

Sri Lanka

Malaysia

Singapore

Maldives

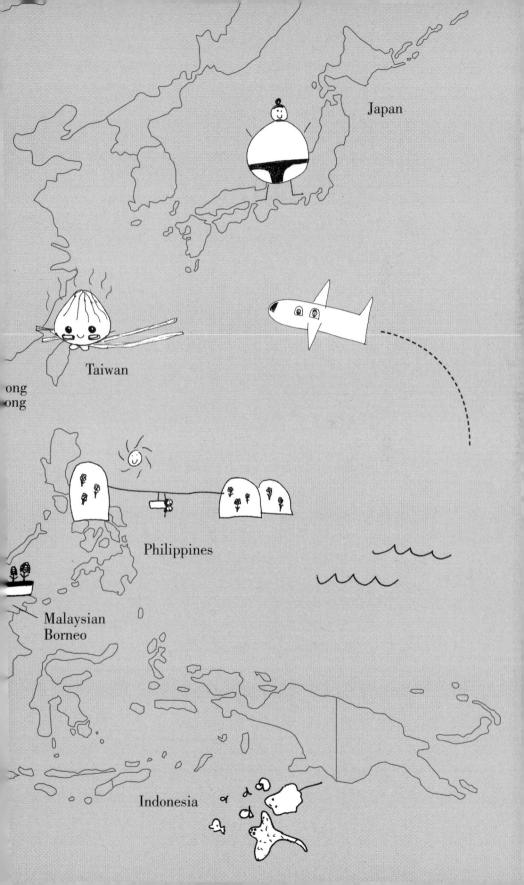

Japan

Taiwan

ong
ong

Philippines

Malaysian
Borneo

Indonesia

Contents

Prologue

'Come on, Mum, please? You know you can do it,' Emmie begged as we stood in the dust on a mountaintop somewhere on Bohol Island in the Philippines.

It was a hot, cloudless day. Under the sharp sunshine, our faces were red and sweaty and our hair stuck to our cheeks in thin, wet strips. We were here only because our sneaky tricycle driver had taken an unscheduled turn up a dirt road. I hadn't been paying attention to where we were going, and now here we were. A zipline predicament.

My little six-year-old had spotted it first, its glistening wires calling her with a metallic hum as they stretched and rattled out across the deep, tree-lined valley.

'Mum, a zipline! Can we, Mum, please? I want to fly.' She was determined and fearless, and wouldn't give up.

'Oh Emmie, I don't think I can. I'm so sorry.' I hated letting her down, but ziplines were not my friends. Riding them meant hanging from wires in a harness far above the earth, feet dangling in the air, my life entrusted to strangers. And everyone makes mistakes.

What was she thinking, this bold little girl of mine? It looked terrifying. I watched as a couple flew out over the nothing below and clattered off into the distance, shrieking in tandem with the metal. Emmie roared with joy and danced from foot to foot, desperately wanting to be out there, too.

'Oh come on, Mum!' She stared at me in frustration. 'I can't go by myself. I'm too little.'

'I can't, Emmie. I'm scared. Please don't beg me.' I wasn't going to fly through the sky suspended from a wire. No way.

She looked up at me and smiled. 'I have an idea, Mum. Whatever you're afraid of, I know what to do. Just yell out your fear while you're flying.'

'What did you say, Emmie?' I asked, wondering if I'd heard right.

'Just yell out your fear while you're flying,' she grinned. 'I'm going to yell "I'm a celebrity, get me out of here" and you can yell out your fear and make it go away. Simple!' She shrugged as if she had it all sorted out.

Maybe she did. If I yelled my fear to the void of the valley, could I free myself from it? Release it into the air and let it go? This might be a good idea. Maybe I could do this for her. And for me.

But what *was* I afraid of? Why was I holding myself back? It wasn't the height and the flying that was stopping me; my fear

12

was buried deep: all my doubts and weaknesses, my sadness, failures and mistakes. My fear of being less-than, that the nastiness at home would never stop, that I'd never be able to give Emmie the life I wanted to. The fear and regret that randomly popped into my head to keep me awake at night.

Yell out my fears? I'd locked them away to help me survive. Did I really want to release them?

We were only a few weeks into our travels, Emmie and me. It was our big adventure, one year of backpacking through Asia, spending every day together—valuable, precious time that we couldn't get at home. This time, together, was my chance to show Emmie who I was—who I *really* was: brave, fun and up for anything … not just the mum who rushed off to work each day and came home late at night, tired and feeling old.

I wanted the old me back. I needed Emmie to see that I was strong, and that I would do anything for her. And that I didn't let fear stop me.

I sighed. 'I seriously cannot believe I am doing this but … yes, okay, let's do it.' I gave in, and her face lit up.

'Thank you, Mum, thank you! You're the best, I love you.' She threw her arms around my waist, grabbed some pesos from my bag and raced over to buy the tickets before I could chicken out. I reluctantly followed her, signed the indemnity forms and chucked my bag into the tricycle. We joined the small queue to the hut where the zipline began.

Hand in hand we waited, watching people shoot out into the air, screaming as the world dropped away. Before I knew it, we were waved over. It was our turn to fly.

We took off our shoes and stepped into a harness. My legs were shaking as I lay down in a long bag with Emmie by my side, the poor little thing squashed in beside me. We were flying Superman-style: horizontal, vulnerable and totally at the mercy of the metal.

'Are you okay, Mum?' Emmie laughed, poking my weak spots. 'Are you scared? Are you crying?'

Three men strapped us in, connected the bag and the wires, and clipped the straps together. Snap. Click. Laugh.

'Are you sure the wires are strong enough? Did you double-check everything? *Are we safe?*' I was desperate in the final seconds, and Emmie loved it. The men laughed kindly and reassured me as they strapped our shoes to the outside of the bag and counted down.

'Three, two, one … goodbye, mama, goodbye, baby,' and they howled as they set us free.

The whizzing and whirring of the wires surrounded us as we slipped over the platform's edge and dropped into nothingness. My heart froze and I whimpered, clutching the straps in terror.

Emmie was ecstatic, her arms outstretched as we soared out over the valley. 'I'm a celebrity, get me out of heeeeeeeeeeeere,' she yelled, euphoric.

Then, it was my turn. With my heart pounding, I thought of home, of being alone and trying to do it all, and as we flew through the sky, I sobbed out my fear: 'I'M NOT GOOD ENOUGH.'

But as soon as I said it, I knew it wasn't true. Emmie was right! Yelling my fear out loud—not just saying it to myself, in my head— showed me how wrong it was. I didn't need to be afraid.

I could do anything. I already did. I didn't have anything to be ashamed of.

I might be a solo mum, but I am just as good as anyone else.
I might be alone, but I am strong.
I might be scared, but I am determined.
I might be hurt, but I am healing.

Emmie pumped the air with her fists. 'You yelled it, Mum! You did it! You're free and flying!'

She flapped her arms in the air as we returned across the valley to the mountainside where we'd started. We were hauled up out of the harness, and we hugged with huge smiles.

This was the moment that I learned the first lesson of my adventures with my wise little girl, Emmie, who loved me no matter what: I was good enough—and I always had been.

CHAPTER 1

Leaving the path

I was drowning at home. I was a solo mum pretending I had everything under control while I sank under the weight of anxiety, insecurity and an overwhelming fear that I was disconnected from my daughter. I constantly searched for ways to change our life, but I was stuck. And I had brought us here.

My path had been the one most followed. I finished school, graduated from university and worked in the city along with everyone else. Society said that stability, conformity and equity were what mattered in life, and I didn't know any different. The checklist of achievements was clear: a steady job, marriage, a mortgage, children, holidays once a year and, finally, retirement after 40 years of working, paying bills and meeting deadlines. Then it would be time to enjoy life, to travel in a campervan or finally explore the world. That is, of course, if you were still alive, mobile, married and had enough money. These were the goals of the 'burbs—and no one seemed to question them.

I grew up in the sunshine of Sydney's Sutherland Shire. It is a beautiful part of the world, with a coastline of bays and beaches, the Royal National Park, rivers and waterways—and the Lucas Heights Nuclear Reactor.

We lived in Woronora, in a two-storey brick home that to me seemed like a palace. We had swings and a slippery dip, a trampoline and a huge slope in the backyard that was perfect for a slip and slide. My sister, Ren, is two years younger than me, and we both went to Woronora River Primary, a tiny school set in the bush across the river from our house. Each morning to get to school, we would walk down our hill and over the little wooden footbridge, where we would look up towards home and see Mum out on our balcony, waving a huge tablecloth for us to spot. In the afternoons, we ran around with the neighbourhood kids, swimming or roaming through the bush, climbing trees and making hide-outs in caves. We jumped from the footbridge into the river, paddled canoes and hiked along the big, green water pipeline to the Needles swimming hole, where we'd catapult from a rope swing into cold, deep water. We came home when the streetlights were turned on or when we heard Mum yelling that dinner was ready.

The beach was a big part of our life, and on weekends Mum and Dad would pack up the umbrella and esky and we would head off to Cronulla, spending the whole day in the surf, only being called in to have sunscreen rubbed all over us every few hours. We joined Nippers at Wanda Surf Life Saving Club, learned to body surf, were dumped by breakers and stung by bluebottles—

classic Aussie beach days. After, Ren and I would wait in the car with a packet of chips and a lemonade each while Mum and Dad had a schooner or two in the local beer garden. It was a simple childhood, when all I cared about was my family and spending time together, those precious moments before I realised what was outside the beautiful bubble.

At high school I made my closest friends, especially Jacqui, who I met in Year 7. She was tall, pretty and smart, and the boys she ignored called her an ice queen. I was her naughty sidekick, getting into trouble for talking and laughing too much and not turning up for class. As we got older, we drank Cinzano and smoked cigarettes on her back deck when her mum was away, spending our days lazing on the beach and our nights sneaking into pubs using the fake IDs we made with the council library's colour photocopier. It was the best time of our high-school life.

For all my naughtiness, I did well in school and went off to study journalism at the University of Canberra, living on campus and driving home most weekends. After uni, I moved back to Sydney and worked in public relations. There were lots of us from school and uni working in the city, and we embraced our new independence, meeting up for after-work drinks and carrying our heavy laptops and chunky mobile phones with us to show how special we were.

Three years later, after hearing her sister Karen's stories about backpacking around the world, Jacqui and I quit our jobs and set off to explore Asia and the Middle East. For some reason we decided to start our adventures on remote Nias Island in Sumatra, and there wasn't an easy way to get there. From Singapore we took a ferry to the Indonesian island of Batam, intending to fly onward until the bloke at the ticket office told us a plane had crashed the week before.

'But don't worry,' he reassured us. 'Only the air hostess died.'

We opted for the boat instead. For fifteen hours, we sat in the rain on bags of produce at the back of an old cargo vessel, drinking mini bottles of red wine we'd sneaked off our Egypt Air flight and chain-smoking in fear. Passengers were crammed in under the deck with livestock and supplies for the islands, and the army boarded in the dead of night. It was an extreme start to our adventure.

This was the trip that ignited my love of travel. I tasted the freedom of being out in the world, of not being restricted by timelines or responsibilities. It was a striking contrast to home. This rugged journey through wild Indonesia, Turkey, Syria, Jordan and Egypt changed my life. Months stretched out ahead with nothing to do but explore; it was life scraped right down to basics. Spending almost every day in nature made us strong and healthy (if occasionally hungover). We all looked the same in our backpacker clothes, and without any immediate social clues, everyone was equal. We were just a community of kids playing, learning, having fun and occasionally calling home. There was no social media, and we were all the better for it.

I swore I'd leave my corporate life and suburban rules when I returned to Sydney. Travelling had shown me that there was so much more. I applied for a working visa in Ireland, where I lived with Jacqui for six months, and then worked for an eccentric film producer in the United States while he was involved in a court case with Sony Corporation over the rights to the James Bond franchise. I lived at the Beverly Wilshire near Rodeo Drive and had meetings in the bathroom of his suite while he ran the taps to hide our conversations, convinced Sony had bugged his room. On the way home, I spent four months with Ren backpacking through Italy,

Prague, Germany and India, meeting Pope John Paul II and succumbing to Delhi Belly.

When I returned to Sydney, I got a public relations job with a shipping company, and when one of its vessels rescued 433 refugees from a sinking fishing boat off the coast of Australia (an event that became known as the Tampa Crisis), I managed the company's media and communication. I was then transferred to the head office in Oslo, Sweden, to develop a global crisis communication strategy and spent my weekends exploring Scandinavia. On the way home, I met up with Jacqui's sister Karen, our friend George and their mates in Unawatuna, Sri Lanka. We swam in the ocean at midnight, ate jumbo prawns on the beach and lazed under the sun. I then set off alone into the mountains, sitting in the doorway of the blue train with locals, climbing Little Adam's Peak and finding happiness in solitude.

When I returned to Australia, I did what everyone else was doing and went straight back into corporate life. I had to earn a living and didn't consider that there might be another way. I stayed on this path for the next fourteen years, and while I worked hard I felt like I was just doing the same old thing over and over. I still needed to travel, though, and I took as much leave as I could.

It was a good life. I was healthy, fortunate, had well-paying jobs and lots of friends. I bought an apartment in Surry Hills and threw parties every month. We had picnics, days at the races and sparkling afternoons drinking champagne on Sydney Harbour. We could do anything we wanted. But ... when the excitement died down, or in the early morning, I wanted to be somewhere else.

I pretended that money and fancy things were important. After all, they seemed to be to everyone else, so they should be to me, too, right? Look good, buy expensive things, make life seem amazing and effortless. I craved freedom, but I replaced it with stability and toed the line. I paid my mortgage, worked on my career and hoped for love.

For a while, we were a tight little gang: me, Jacqui, Karen and George. We all lived near each other in Surry Hills and would meet in one of the pubs on our way home from work almost every night. My friends became my family. We did everything together. When Jacqui moved overseas and Karen coupled up, it was me and George, out at the pub, catching up after work or lying on the couch, watching sport on TV.

In my early thirties, I began a relationship with a bloke who I thought was the one for me, coincidentally on the same night George met the man who became her husband. Looking back, my relationship was doomed from the start. I should have walked away after our awful first date, but the crush I'd had on him since high school blinded me. I don't know why he stayed.

I truly loved this man, no matter his faults, and I would have done anything for him. A few years into our relationship, we bought an apartment back in the Shire and returned to the ocean and the big sky. I thought this was my future. But while we spent time with his friends, I slowly isolated myself from mine, embarrassed by how he treated me in front of them. And it was worse when we were alone.

I remember him saying the same nasty things over and over to me, until I started to believe them. I stayed quiet when he told his friends that he supported me financially. I wanted to make him happy, and if he needed to build his ego to do that, then so be it.

I lost my confidence, picking up any scraps of kindness he would throw on the floor in the hope that one day things would change. I'm not blameless. In times of sadness, wine was my friend.

In retrospect, all I can see is a young woman in love who had all her joy drained away.

When we'd first started seeing each other, it seemed like we had so much in common, but we didn't really. He wasn't interested in travelling, and he didn't care for weekends away unless it was with his mates. I was disappointed, but it didn't stop me. I kept using whatever leave I had to travel—to Mongolia with George and to Singapore and Bangkok to meet up with Jacqui—but I would have loved for him to come, too.

I was in Thailand when I suspected that I was pregnant. I had won the trip in a raffle at Cronulla RSL, and I had wanted him to come, but he wouldn't. Instead, Ren had flown over from Dubai to join me. Afterwards, I flew to Singapore to visit Jacqui and her partner Jav for a few days.

I'd been feeling a little odd in Thailand and I was still light-headed in Singapore, so I walked down to Great World City while Jacqui was at work and bought a pregnancy test. I'd been diagnosed with severe polycystic ovarian syndrome many years earlier and told it would be nearly impossible to conceive naturally, but I just had a feeling. I told myself how ridiculous I was being, but I wanted to take the test.

I waited until Jacqui and Jav got home from work, and we drank some bubbles on their balcony overlooking the Singapore skyline while I prepared to wee on the stick. I was so nervous! Finally I built up the courage, and they cheered me on while I went into the bathroom, did a wee and walked out—totally forgetting to use the stick! Nerves, I tell you.

When I finally managed to do it properly, we watched as two blue lines appeared. I was pregnant. I changed my flight and raced home, excited to see his reaction. I cried when I showed him the test, standing on our balcony looking out towards the ocean. He gave me a huge hug and told me how happy he was. He was so supportive and caring during the pregnancy that my friends said they were seeing his good side, softened by becoming a dad.

On a hot January day, our beautiful Emily Rebel exploded out of me with bright blue feet, alert eyes and a puffy face. She had been the wrong way around, her spine grinding on mine for an agonising twelve hours while I turned into a wild beast, screaming, vomiting and abusing the doctor for not giving me drugs. Now she was here—our little miracle—and I was in love.

My memory of this beautiful moment is tinged with sadness. As I lay there with my little girl in my arms, exhausted after the birth, I remember her dad looking at my stomach with distaste and asking me if there was another one in there. I remember my heart freezing as he told me I looked fat.

A few days later, we carried our Emmie home from hospital. I was expecting to be a happy family of three, but her dad was withdrawn and went straight back to work. I was left alone to figure out how to look after this tiny baby who never slept.

I failed in my attempts to affix nappies, my haphazard constructions hanging lopsided and loose. My boobs leaked everywhere, and I mistook the sounds of precious milk dripping on the floor for rain on the roof. I hand-pumped minute amounts and then knocked the bottles over while trying to seal them, spilling the liquid gold.

I was terrified of hurting her. I feared dropping her, or stumbling and losing my grip and sending her flying to the floor. I took the stairs sitting down, scooting one by one with Emmie in my arms to avoid hurting my precious girl.

That summer was a scorcher. Temperatures topped 40 degrees daily, the sun was like a laser and the air felt like hot slaps on my body. I was hot, anxious and alone. Too scared to go outside by myself, I stayed in with the air-conditioning cranked as high as it could go. A few weeks after the birth, I took Emmie to hospital because of a rash and nonstop screaming, but when the doctor saw me, he said I was the one who needed looking after, and I finally had a good sleep in the chair next to her bed.

That first month, Emmie's dad slept in the spare room and disappeared on weekends, leaving me alone for days. Since he parked his car in the garage, I had to find parking on the street and whenever I managed to leave the house, I had to wait until my car cooled down enough to put Emmie inside. I left handwritten love notes out for him from me and Emmie, but they went unanswered. During the few times he was home, we argued. The girls I'd spent most of my time with over the last few years, who'd been his friends first, stayed away.

The second month, he stopped talking to me.

Somehow, stupidly, I remained optimistic. I was hormonal, and a new baby is difficult for all relationships. *We can get through this*, I thought.

One day when Emmie was three months old, he told me he'd realised he had never loved me at all and that he was leaving. I followed him down the hallway. 'What about Emmie?' I cried in disbelief. 'You can't leave us, I don't know what I'm doing.'

He looked back at me from the front door.

'Please don't go,' I begged, fear sinking in. Living in a home with a newborn and a barely-there partner was excruciating, but in that minute the unknown seemed worse.

He turned and walked out.

And just like that, Emmie and I were on our own.

I allowed myself tears, but I refused to break. I knew Emmie and I were better off without him, and to be honest, my pride hurt more than my heart. I'd already been doing everything by myself anyway; it wasn't like much would change. In fact, there would be more peace and happiness in our home now that he was gone. As I heard him drive away, I picked up Emmie and held her in my arms.

'It's just us, baby,' I told her. 'We can do it. We are going to be so happy together.'

⌣

Now I was officially a solo mum, trying to learn on the job but with a deep sadness heavy in my belly. And that wasn't the worst of it. Soon I heard rumours circulating about me: that I'd taken his money, that we'd never even been in a relationship and had only bought our home as 'friends'. They were hurtful, unnecessary and entirely untrue. I hated that people were talking about me when I was already down, and it made me feel isolated and like an outcast in my own community.

Thankfully, I had my family around me, and new and old friends appeared like magic to keep me going. Mum, Dad and Ren would pop in, Aunty Linda and Uncle Bruce came past with pasta and meatballs, and friends from school, mother's group and work called and visited to check on me.

Every time I took Emmie for a check-up, the local doctor would tell me, 'You're doing a good job, you're a good mum,' and I'd cry because that's what I needed to hear. My heart was broken, not so much from Emmie's dad leaving, but from sadness and isolation.

I questioned myself constantly and felt very alone. It was the hardest thing I had ever been through.

After a month of readjusting, I felt like I needed to mark an end-point to that life and a starting point for our new one. I had a daughter relying on me, and I needed to be strong.

I called my mum for advice. 'Mum, I need to get away. I think Emmie and I will go to Fiji. What do you reckon?'

'Well, if you're going, I'm coming, too,' she said immediately. 'I can help with Emmie, and you can rest.'

Two weeks later, we walked through Sydney Airport with Emmie strapped to my chest, her little fists pumping. It was her first flight, and it all went well until she did a massive poo on descent that leaked all over my white pants (who wears white pants on a flight with a baby?), and we later found out she was the wrong way around in the bassinet. Regardless, we all arrived safely in Nadi and set off on a two-hour bus ride south to the Coral Coast.

The holiday was just what I needed. Every morning, before the heat of the day set in, I would take Emmie swimming in the huge pool just outside our room. The staff would watch from the balcony as my tiny baby happily kicked her legs in the water. After all that exercise and a quick shower, she would fall into a deep sleep, something she rarely did at home.

Our days were spent swimming and lying on the grass, resting and watching the palm leaves swaying above, with Emmie, as always, smiling and giggling. Mum patiently looked after her while I swam, slept and sorted through my emotions. I quickly realised that feeling bitter was only going to hurt me and Emmie, and for every nasty person at home, there were two kind people in my life. I would focus on that.

Mum went home, and Emmie and I had a few days together at the resort on our very first solo trip, just being together with a little help from Suri, a Fijian nanny who helped us for a few hours a day. I was so in love with Emmie, and while I was a little scared of what was ahead, I knew we could do it.

Back from Fiji, we put our home on the market and it quickly sold. I rented a small apartment near the beach, and when Emmie was six months old, I returned to work in the city. I desperately wanted more time with her, but we needed the money.

Two days each week, Mum and Dad would drive up from their place down the coast to help with Emmie, taking care of her while I was at work. I enrolled her in long day care for the other three days, dropping her off on my way to work and picking her up afterwards. It was a long time for her to be in care, but I didn't think there were any other options.

Being a solo mum brought more challenges than simply looking after Emmie alone, supporting us both financially and trying to get her dad involved in her life. I also found that, whether knowingly or not, many people look down on single mums. Sometimes, friends would describe a woman condescendingly—'she's a single mum'—and then look at me and hurriedly say, 'Oh, but you're different. You're not like the other single mums.' What was that supposed to mean? It made me feel terrible. I was still me, whether or not I had a partner. Why did it matter?

But I felt the judgment, and it made me determined that Emmie and I would be just as good as everyone else—and that meant buying a house. Sadly, this meant selling my awesome city apartment, which I've always regretted. But when Emmie was two, I was able to buy a house for us with the money I got from the sale. Our 'new' home was old and draughty, but it had a leafy backyard, was a ten-minute walk to the beach and you could barely hear the cars on the main road outside our windows. Best of all, it was ours.

Was it the right decision to stay in the Shire? Probably not, but I just needed to keep the cogs moving. Any movement was progress, no matter which direction I was going in.

It's a parochial place, the Shire, with the ocean as its heartbeat and footy in its blood. The sense of community is strong here, and the desire to belong is stronger. People say you need your passport to get in, and once you make it in, you never leave. It is kind of like that, and it can be comforting or suffocating. As much as I loved it, and the many kind, helpful and supportive people in this little world, I often felt like I couldn't breathe. I felt constant anxiety from my relationship with Emmie's dad, a nasty undercurrent of rumours in the neighbourhood and a general sense that I was being looked down on by former friends and acquaintances. Although we travelled a lot—to Disneyland, Fiji, Barbados and Singapore—we had an old house and an old car, and I was a solo mum, and that just didn't fit the Shire mould.

I was always coming up with a new plan to show everyone that I didn't fit the stereotype they'd boxed me into. 'I've decided to get a pool!' I announced to the mums at Emmie's soccer game.

'We're buying a new car!' I told everyone the next week and started test-driving Jeeps and four-wheel drives, before sticking with my old Toyota Corolla, the most reliable old chunk of junk ever.

Then finally, 'I'm getting a new kitchen!' as I checked out my friends' designer kitchens and picked their brains. A butler's pantry! A serving window! Eventually, it expanded into quotes for a total house renovation.

But something always held me back, and I thank the universe for that. Maybe deep down, I worried that I would spend all that money and still feel the same unhappiness, but with nothing left in the bank.

⌣

What I needed the most was more time with Emmie. We were hardly seeing each other. I was leaving for work before 7.00 am every morning and coming home after 8.00 pm at night. That's not unusual if you're in a corporate job or run your own business; most of us work long hours. But when you have a small child and you're a solo parent, it's just not good for your heart or your baby.

When Emmie was four years old, I switched her out of long day care to a centre that was smaller and closer to our home, but had limited hours. Someone had to cover the remaining hours while I was at work, but I worried about paying $25 an hour for a babysitter. I overheard a group of mums talking about hiring live-in au pairs, and we had a spare room, so within weeks Coco, our first au pair, arrived from France. It was fabulous to have her with us. She—and later Viktoria from Germany—felt like a younger sister and it was nice to have someone else around. The girls got to experience life in Sydney, came on holidays with us, and just hung out with us like a little family. I trusted them completely.

All the while, I was working hard to earn money to buy things we didn't need to show people that I was good enough, while trying to make more time to spend with Emmie. It was all counterproductive. No matter what anyone says, single mum or not, it is not possible to do it all, and we are denying ourselves valuable time with our families by trying to make it happen.

30

Then, in 2015, my heart stopped when my friend George passed away. George and I had spent so much time together during the previous ten years, though a little less when we both had children and lived a few hours apart. She and her family had visited us in Cronulla, and we'd been up to stay with her up the coast, the kids running wild on the beach and around the lake near their house. Many of my best memories are with George. She had a huge appetite for adventure and was up for anything. The vision of her in a pink fleece running through a field with yaks is imprinted on my brain, and always makes me smile. She loved travelling and was so much fun to be around, whether it was being dirty and freezing while camping in a tent by Khövsghöl Nuur lake in Mongolia, lying on the couch watching her beloved Waratahs play rugby or running around on the beach with her gorgeous daughters. Before she got sick, we would chat on the phone almost every day as we drove to work. I never for a second thought she would not be in my life.

When she died, it broke my heart, and it became my catalyst for action. I was missing out on being with Emmie because of money, because of work. It wasn't right, the way our life was. Emmie and I didn't even know each other because we spent so much time apart. I was terrified that I was going to die without showing Emmie anything except my back as I ran off to work each day. I had to change everything, but I didn't know how.

'The most important thing is that you and Emmie are happy. What makes you happy?' my friend Jenny asked one day, as we played with Emmie in the park. I was trying to figure out how to change my life to spend more time with her, which seemed impossible.

'Being with Emmie and travelling,' I answered quickly. It was that simple. 'We're at our best when we're travelling together. There's no work to keep me away from her, and no deadlines or things we have to do. It's just us having fun.'

'Well, why don't you just do that then? Go travelling together?' Jenny asked.

I paused as my mind processed how absolutely simple and perfect this idea was.

'Jenny ... that's it. Emmie and I can go travelling together through Asia. It's friendly, it's safe, it's affordable. I'll use my kitchen money to fund it and rent out the house. I think this is the way!'

I called Jacqui and filled her in. 'I'm thinking of travelling with Emmie for a year. What do you reckon? Could it work?' I asked, forming a plan as the idea started to sink in.

'Of course!' she said instantly, always my cheer squad. 'You can do whatever you want. You just have to make it happen.'

It was an easy decision to use the money I'd saved to travel. I'd been trying to spend it for so long—on a pool, a car, a kitchen—and I never could. But now, I knew what the money was for. I reckoned that it would last me about a year.

For the first time in a long time, I was excited. A whole year together? What family wouldn't dream of that? And that's what we were—a little family of two, trying to find our way.

It was July 2015.

⌣

I was so keen to talk to Emmie about this new idea. I knew that because she was only five years old, she might not understand it entirely, but what she wanted more than anything else was for us to be together, and this was how I could make it happen.

She was now in kindergarten at the local Catholic school and was mostly looked after by Viktoria before and after school. 'Mummy, can you pick me up from school?' she would ask.

'Mummy, can you do reading at school?'

'Mummy, can I have a friend over for a playdate?'

I wasn't there, so the answer was always no, and it broke my heart. But now I had a solution.

'Emmie, you know I want to spend more time with you, and we want to be together? Well, I have a plan!' I announced carefully, knowing that she had to want to do it, too.

'What is it, Mama?' she asked. 'Are you going to stop your job?'

'Yes, well, kind of,' I said. 'You know how we have the most fun, exciting holidays together and how we always have a good time? What about if we went on holiday for an extra-long time? Travelling together and having adventures. How does that sound to you?'

'That sounds great, Mama. I just want to be together.'

'Of course, Emmie! We will be together every day.'

'Yes, Mummy, that's what I want,' she said happily.

She ran into her room and came out dragging her carry-on bag behind her. 'I'm ready to go!' she said with a grin.

We wouldn't get a new car or a pool. We would never have a new kitchen. But we didn't really want those things anyway. We would spend our money travelling for a year in Asia. I couldn't think of a better way to spend it. We were going to be together.

CHAPTER 2

Our little big
adventure

I was in. Emmie was in. Now I just had to sort everything out.

I started planning our adventure but didn't tell anyone. For now, this plan was Emmie's and mine, and anyway, I was sure everyone would think it was yet another one of my big ideas that would never happen.

This secret project was better than anything I'd ever worked on. I made lists of what I needed to do and I started ticking them off. I whizzed through my work and researched home rental prices and storage sheds, calling real estate agents and insurance companies while hiding in halls and meeting rooms. I discovered that I could teach Emmie through our state's Distance Education Program, and I signed up, with visions of being an inspiring teacher and Emmie an attentive student. I dreamed of our time together as I sorted out our flights, and I had faith we would figure it out as we went along.

I focused on what needed to be done to get us onto the plane out of Sydney, but that was it. Part of the reason we were going was to break free from routine and restrictions, so why would I plan a detailed adventure with bookings and deadlines to lock us down? I wanted us to be free.

I made sure that Emmie's dad was okay with me taking her on this adventure. They didn't see each other much, so Emmie travelling for a while wouldn't be a big change for either of them. I set up FaceTime, email and other ways to communicate while we were away.

I picked a date for us to leave: Monday, 1 February 2016. It was just before school started for the new year, and it gave us all of January to spend with family and friends before we set off. Date chosen, I slowly started to share our plans. I felt most nervous telling my parents and sister because they absolutely adore Emmie, but, as usual, they were super supportive and the blow was softened when I reassured them we could meet up in Asia whenever they wanted.

Many of my friends seemed amused, and I understood why. It was a big dream to drop on them, and after all my talk of renovations and swimming pools and new cars, I wouldn't have been surprised if no one had believed me until we'd flown off. My big concern was whether my new friendships would survive.

'Oh, don't worry about that,' said Alison, a friend I'd made through Emmie's preschool. 'Nothing changes in the suburbs. It will all be the same when you get back.'

She was right. Nothing would change.

That was one of the reasons why we had to go.

⌣

Introducing Emmie to adventurous travel had always been my goal. Now that she was five, I felt she could handle more than a resort stay. It was time to show her the rawness of the real world, where it's uncomfortable and challenging but oh so rewarding. I wanted her to be curious, to develop a desire to explore and to grow with an open mind. I needed to get her out of the bubble. I knew we'd see some things that might upset her, but it was important that she was aware of how fortunate she was, and I wanted her to develop empathy for others.

'Emmie, when we're travelling, it's really important to learn about other people and how they live,' I explained. 'It will kind of be like visiting new friends who have really interesting lives that are different to ours. Sometimes we might see things that will make us sad, but we're going to learn a lot and have so much fun together.'

'Mummy, why would we be sad?' she asked straight away.

'Well hon, some families and children don't have much at all—not even toys, and the children can't go to school. You might get sad because it's not fair. We are so lucky, Emmie.'

'Okay, Mummy, I understand. As long as we're together it will be okay, and maybe we can help people, too.' She thought a bit. 'I don't know if I'll eat all the food. Will we see lots of animals? Will we swim? What will we do?' She was so excited and completely accepting. She knew we were going to be together, and that was the most important thing for her.

'We'll do whatever we like! We will move when we want to move, stop where we want to stop. No rules, no plans, just nice and free. And we'll have every day together.'

37

'No rules?' Her little eyes lit up.

Oops. 'Well, yes, some rules, you know, but we're going to be pretty easy. It's going to be a whole different life. We are going to learn about the world by being in it.'

Before we set off on our big trip, we needed to dip our toes into backpacking, to make sure Emmie was okay with it and have a little practice. It had been a few years since I'd bumbled my way around budget-style, so it was a test run for both of us. Malaysian Borneo was calling my name, and the lure of big-nosed proboscis monkeys and beautiful endangered orangutans sealed the deal.

'Emmie, what do you think about orangutans, jungles, caves and giant bugs?' I asked as I searched for flights.

'I love it, Mummy. I can't wait!'

I booked our flights on the cheap, using my Qantas points, and we trotted off to our local Kathmandu store to grab hiking shorts and shoes, drink bottles and packing cubes.

We packed up the backpack that I'd taken on my first backpacking trip with Jacqui in 1997. That old backpack had seen a lot, like remote islands in Indonesia and ancient ruins in Syria. It was with me in Jordan when we learned of Princess Diana's death, and in Egypt when we narrowly missed the terrorist attack at Luxor. It had been there for boozy nights, new friendships and romances on the road, and now it was coming with me on an entirely different adventure. Hoisting it onto my back with my five-year-old daughter by my side was a dream come true. Emmie was jumping all over the place with excitement and couldn't wait to leave.

'We're going to Borneo with no money!' she would tell people. Well, she was close.

We set off together on our little big adventure one morning in October, arriving at Sydney Airport loaded up with our packs. The terminal was busy with the energy of thousands of travellers finding their flights, and we scanned the board and found our check-in counter.

'This is it,' I told her, holding hands as we waited. 'Our first big adventure. Are you ready?'

'Yes, I am. I'm so excited, Mama. Can I watch a movie on the plane, please?' Flying with kids is so much easier once they can use the in-flight entertainment, that's for sure.

We arrived in Kuching, Sarawak, after three flights and a twelve-hour transit in Hong Kong. We took a bus to the waterfront, found our room in the budget Tune Hotel and collapsed on the bed.

'Mum, I'm hungry! Where's the phone so I can order room service?' Emmie asked. Our tiny room didn't even have a phone, and there was definitely no room service, but I told her to search for it while I giggled to myself.

'Mum, did you know this? There's no phone! Or TV!' She looked at me in shock.

'Honey, we're backpackers now, we don't need those things,' I told her. 'Come on, let's explore and find some street food.'

Off we went, holding hands as we wandered down the hill to the bustling waterfront. The Sarawak River softly curves through the city, surrounded by colonial buildings, a paved esplanade with brightly lit food stalls, souvenir stands, and parks filled with modern art and cat statues. We bought laksa and rice and sat at the edge of the river, watching the sun set over the stunning golden-roofed Astana. Groups of children sang and danced to music from their old boom boxes, riverboats floated by, and boatmen sailed from jetty to jetty in traditional wooden *penambang* boats.

'Well, Mummy, here we are,' Emmie said. 'So far, I've learned that we do not have room service, Kuching loves cats, I don't like laksa and the city is pretty. It's been a good first day.'

Each morning at the hotel, we sat at a little outdoor area overlooking other balconies and eateries and scoffed breakfast packets of chicken and rice before setting out for the day. We visited the Semenggoh Nature Reserve, an orangutan rehabilitation centre famous for the exploits of its dominant male, Ritchie, who had a habit of chasing visitors and park rangers. We spent hours on the Kuching waterfront, finding cat statues and exploring museums and side streets. We took a small boat out to Bako National Park and hiked through the mangroves, spotting wild boars, a bright green Bornean pit viper, and proboscis monkeys eating berries from trees lining the shore. Baby macaques chased Emmie and tried to grab her pink shoelaces, while the bigger monkeys tried to take our lunch. We visited the Sarawak Cultural Village and learned all about the tribes of Malaysian Borneo, some still living by traditional rules in longhouses under the guidance of a chief.

We ate at Top Spot Food Court, a giant prawn marking its location on the roof of a carpark, and sipped sugarcane juice while Emmie wrote in her journal. Emmie gobbled down colourful traditional Sarawak cake called *kek lapis* that we bought from local women selling it in big plastic crates on the side of the street, and we hunted for more. We discovered that we could spend $10 each to hang at the Hilton Hotel pool across the road from our budget room, and spent a hot afternoon lazing in a bit of luxury.

'Do you reckon we can do this for longer than a few weeks, Emmie?' I asked.

'Mum, of course.' She waved her arm in my direction. 'We are going on a year of travel, and it's going to be the best thing ever!'

We flew to Gunung Mulu National Park, a UNESCO World Heritage Site in an old-growth tropical rainforest. Our propeller plane dodged towering cumulonimbus clouds as it soared over limestone mountains covered in thick jungle and landed at the tiny Mulu airport.

We arrived at our budget accommodation to be greeted by my first mistake. 'I'm sorry,' said the man at the desk. 'Your booking is for tomorrow. And tonight we are full.'

It was scorching hot, and the other guesthouses right next to the park were small and steamy with only fans in the rooms. I'd seen a fancy hotel in the rainforest as we flew into Mulu and began creating reasons why we needed to stay there instead of the budget spots. *It would be too much for Emmie to stay in a hot room,* I told myself. *She really needs a pool to cool down in.*

I pretended to be reluctant as we took the shuttle over to the Mulu Marriott, knowing full well that if they had a free room I was going to grab it. And I did.

The resort was absolutely stunning, with a beautiful pool, wooden walkways and staff on bikes to deliver guests' bags to luxurious rooms partly hidden in the rainforest. After our forced night's stay, I stopped pretending that we were going back to budget. The Marriott became our home for the next three days. That was a mistake I was so glad I made.

We spent our days hiking through ancient rainforest, exploring enormous caves, discovering giant rhinoceros beetles, canopy walking, and sailing in a longboat up the Melinau River to meet locals living in villages on its banks. Our guide showed us the belian trees that tribes used to make blowpipes, and we fell in love with nature and this slower pace of life.

We were eager to see the bat exodus, when each evening at dusk millions of bats fly out of Deer Cave to hunt for mosquitos. We hiked up to the cave and waited. But, instead of bats, the sky was dark with clouds—and we learned that bats don't like the rain.

'Mummy, can we go back?' Emmie whined an hour later, her snacks gone and no bats on the horizon.

'Okay, let's abandon ship. I don't think any bats will be coming out tonight,' I said, a little worried because it was getting dark and we had a three-kilometre walk back to the park entrance.

'Rejected by bats,' Emmie said sadly as she stood up. 'Okay, let's go. And Mum? We better hurry because the rain has been waiting for us. Goodbye, everyone,' and she waved farewell to the stayers.

As we started walking, splatters of rain splashed our shoulders and quickly became heavier. And where were our rain jackets? In the backpack in our hotel room, of course.

'Oh Emmie, I think we have to run,' I told her. We were already saturated, the temperature had dropped, and the light was fading fast.

'Mummy, will it help if we sing the *Pitch Perfect* songs while we run?' she suggested. We had been watching it most nights on my computer so we knew every single word.

'That's a great idea, Emmie. Let's do it!'

The rain beat down on us, but we held hands and sang those familiar songs over and over while running through the rapidly approaching darkness. We plodded down the mountain, through the jungle and over bubbling rivers until we reached the park office ... which was closed.

We found the security desk, and the kind guard called the Marriott shuttle for us. It arrived in minutes and, back at the resort, we ran through the rain to our room, jumped into a hot shower and then ordered room service for dinner.

I stared at Emmie as she sat on the bed with her wet hair wrapped in a towel, chatting animatedly about our big, wet run down the mountain. It was at this precise moment that I realised my daughter was a trouper. My daughter, with my hair, my nose, and my little toes, also had my spirit. She had my love of adventure, my dig-deep-and-get-it-done attitude, and she would keep on trying and not give up. This was where we needed to be, and I knew we were on the cusp of something even bigger. The door to a fulfilling and exciting life was starting to open for us, and it was up to us to walk through it.

We spent the last days of our trip enjoying a bit more luxury at the gorgeous Shangri-La Tanjung Aru Resort in Kota Kinabalu, swimming and playing together in the sunshine. I reckon I went down the waterslides about twenty times with Emmie, because that's what mums do.

Our practice run was a success. We had passed the test.

It was going to work out. I could feel it.

CHAPTER 3

The positive what-ifs?

Back in Sydney, it was all systems go for our trip. With only a few months before we left, I had a lot to do. People often ask how difficult it was for Emmie and me to travel together for so long. Well, packing up was infinitely harder than walking away, and so much more difficult than the actual travelling. The struggle continued until the day we left. Thankfully, my friend Bec and her family looked after Emmie a few times while I sorted, boxed, packed and threw out our stuff, and she stayed with Mum and Dad as well.

It was ridiculous how much we had, not only the bits and pieces I'd kept for years that we no longer needed, but the multitude of new things, the 'stuff' I'd bought and hardly used. I was amazed at the amount of money I'd wasted and the excess I had, especially the toys and clothes that Emmie hadn't even touched. I found a few pairs of shoes in my cupboard that I'd never worn. The most annoying part was that we did not have money to throw around, and I'd been wasting it.

The difficulty of packing up our life was far outweighed by the freedom I gained with every bit of stuff I removed. Shoes and dresses donated to charity meant goodbye to buying expensive clothes to fit in at places I didn't want to be. Throwing away quotes for a new pool and kitchen meant farewell to spending money on home improvements to try to fit in. Giving away unneeded items I'd collected over the years freed me from the past. Stripping out the house cleared away all the bad juju and pressure I'd put on myself to be different from who I was.

I arranged storage for the few things we were keeping, and sold or gave away the rest—so much of it never used, or even needed. It was liberating! I had an old caravan down the coast that we kept and I stored a few things there. It was a connection to home, and I hoped to rent it out on weekends and holidays while we were gone.

I honestly feel that when you make the right decision, things just fall into place. Opportunities appear, the path smooths, barriers seem to dissolve. I used to force things to happen when they just didn't want to. I would push, strategise and manipulate to get what I wanted. It worked a lot of the time, but it took a lot of effort and sometimes the outcome probably wasn't the best one. Now I've realised that when you're on the right path, everything works out. At least it did for us.

I talked to Emmie's school principal about withdrawing her for a year. I was so, so nervous, and ready to beg and plead our case. Instead, I ended up crying because she was so understanding.

'This is the best childhood experience you can give her,' she told me. 'I think it's wonderful.'

Resigning from my job was even easier. Again, the universe helped out: a restructure was announced, and I had the option of taking another position or resigning. I gave notice and left with relationships intact. Plus, I finished at Christmas and was paid out a four-week notice period.

By December, I was getting down to the nitty-gritty. I organised annual travel insurance, put our private health cover on hold and the local real estate agent took photos of our home and put it online for rent. My friend Anna agreed to borrow our car while we were gone, so I wouldn't have to spend money buying a new one when we came back, and I farmed out my Thermomix, juicer and other good stuff to friends.

I booked one-way tickets to the Philippines, a dream destination of tropical blue water and palm tree-lined white beaches.

'But what if you don't like it?' a friend questioned.

'What if you can't rent out your house?' asked another.

'What if you come back and you can't get a job?'

I knew they meant well, but these questions annoyed me. *What if, what if?* I didn't care about these limiting, negative what-ifs! If I listened to them, we would never get anywhere. Why stay in one place and not do what our hearts and souls were desperate for, just because possibly, potentially, somewhere far in the future, something may not work out?

So often we seem to focus on the reasons why we shouldn't change, putting up barriers to doing what we want to because we don't have a guarantee that everything will work out perfectly. When we consider changing our lives, why are we more inclined to list why our dreams won't work than why they will? That just doesn't make sense.

The what-ifs kept coming.

What if it's too difficult?
What if you get sick?
What if it's not safe?
What if you can't handle it?

I chose not to worry about those pesky negative what-ifs. Why worry about the worst that can happen when you can think about the best instead?

What if we have the time of our lives?
What if everything goes perfectly well?
What if I find happiness?
What if it's the best decision I ever make?

⌣

For so long our trip had seemed far away and then, suddenly, it was the end of the year. I finished work, Emmie finished school, and we spent Christmas with Mum, Dad and Ren. We both had farewell parties with our friends, me at the Opera House and Emmie down at the beach. Then it was January and the countdown to our departure was well and truly on.

I packed up our backpack, starting with the schoolwork sent to us from Distance Education. The multiple blue folders weighed in at five kilos, a quarter of the twenty kilos I could carry easily in my backpack. I shoved them in, grumbling about space, and then added our packing cubes of clothes, toiletries and first-aid supplies, and snorkels and masks.

Finally, I finished packing up our home, and the removalists took off with the things that I felt would take time to buy new when we returned, like our beds, couch and table. The house wasn't rented yet, but I had faith it would all work out. I knew it would work out.

I cleaned and locked up our empty house, and we were on our way. We dropped the car to Anna and met my sister, mum and dad at the Shangri-La Hotel in the city. We spent our last night in rooms overlooking Sydney's Harbour Bridge and Opera House, watching the toy-like green and yellow ferries pulling in and out of Circular Quay. We loved Sydney so much, but we were ready to go.

I felt every single second tick past. I couldn't wait to be free. There were no nerves, no second thoughts, just a tingling of anticipation and a lovely disbelief that this was actually happening.

'Mummy, Mummy, we're leaving today!' Emmie woke me up before the alarm in the morning, bouncing on the bed and ready to get to the airport. This was it! This was our day. It was ridiculous! It was amazing. Our whole world was about to open up.

'Let's get to it, Emmie! Oh my gosh I'm so excited! Are you excited?' I could hardly believe it.

After breakfast—where Emmie lost her front tooth!—we bundled into Mum and Dad's car for a drive through the city to the airport, arriving three hours before our flight time. Getting to the airport on time always worries me, even though I know it's not the end of the world if we miss a flight. It's one of my few travel anxieties and, apart from literally arriving for the flight a day early, I don't know how to make it go away. Once we are checked in,

I feel good, then a little better once we are through immigration and then okay when we are at the gate. By the time we are strapped into our seats, my missing-the-flight nerves disappear and my fear-of-flying nerves take over.

'We're travelling for one year,' Emmie told the Qantas staff as we checked in, and I hoped her excitement and cuteness would get us upgraded. It didn't. They'd seen it all before.

Standing at the departure gate, my mum and dad were in tears, Emmie was a bundle of energy and I was bursting with excitement. I did my best to be sympathetic to their sense of 'ending' while managing my own feelings of a new beginning.

'Stay safe.'

'Have a great time.'

'Call us when you get there.'

'I love you.'

Mum was crying as we turned towards our new life: twelve months with no plans, no expectations and no deadlines. As we walked away, we were leaving what we knew and heading towards a whole new world for the two of us. We were changing everything. It was the moment when we stepped into our dreams. It was one of the best moments of my life.

Now, we were just us and could be defined by our adventures together instead of the kind of family we were, the house we owned or the car we drove. It's hard to describe the immense joy I felt as we walked through departures. It was an overwhelming sense of freedom and happiness. All the worries, commitments, timetables and to-do lists, all the things I should have done, could have done, would have done, were stripped away, and suddenly I had space in my mind. Our future was full of possibility and opportunity. It was everything, and it was beautiful.

'Emmie!' I beamed as I grabbed her little hand. 'We're going! I can't believe it!'

'Mummy, we are going to be together! I'm so happy!' She looked at me with sparkling eyes, and then burst into tears.

'Oh honey, are you okay?' I knelt down and gave her a hug.

'I didn't like seeing Nanny crying,' she said.

'Don't worry,' I told her. 'We can FaceTime Nanny from the lounge. You'll see her in a few minutes.'

She sparked up straight away, and we set off to immigration and customs.

'Mummy, we're doing it,' Emmie said. 'Just you and me together. Every single day. Now can we go to the Qantas lounge please?'

'Ha, of course. Let's go, ladybug.'

And off we went.

CHAPTER 4

And here we go

Emmie and I sat side by side on the plane, grinning the biggest smiles of anyone on the flight, our matching Bon Voyage eye masks propped on top of our heads. We couldn't sit still, we had ants in our pants with the anticipation of taking off. We chattered away, made up silly songs, giggled, wiggled and held hands, and told each other how excited we were to finally be together and how much we loved each other.

I'd had a celebratory glass of bubbles and a cheese plate in the Qantas lounge while Emmie had tucked into some ice-cream and said more goodbyes to Mum on the phone. I knew this would be our last visit to the lounge—it was one of the lifestyle perks I was saying goodbye to now I was officially unemployed—but it felt right to be flying Qantas out of Australia on the first leg of our trip.

The start of our adventure was kind of a soft launch. I'd chosen the Philippines because of its thousands of gorgeous islands scattered across the Pacific Ocean and South China Sea. I thought its tropical vibe would suit our celebratory beginning.

We had three-month visas and would spend the first twelve weeks of our trip roaming around and exploring the islands, but that was as far as my planning went. After all the rushing around and farewelling and packing, I was pretty tired. I felt we'd need to land with little fuss and spend a few days recharging, so while I was working and had the money, I'd booked us two nights at the fancy Shangri-La resort in Cebu. It was our first stop, and we would use the time to reset and plan our next move in a bit of luxury. Philippines, we were on our way!

The plane sped down the runway, and Emmie and I held hands and started a ritual that we would continue for every flight.

'And here we go,' we said together as we lifted off into the sky.

We landed in Manila late at night, commemorating our arrival with our new little saying as the wheels touched down: 'And here we are.'

We connected to another flight, on Cebu Pacific airline, where they played Top 40 hits as we boarded and held giveaways during the flight. Emmie won a pink travel wallet, and we were feeling good when we landed on the island of Cebu. As we walked out of the airport into the steaming hot night air, Emmie grabbed my arm.

'Mum, that's our names,' she said excitedly, pointing to a man holding a sign.

'Really? What? Where?' I sceptically scanned the crowd waiting near the exit. Yep, there were our names! Evie and Emmie Farrell written on a sign held by a man in a suit and a driver's cap. The resort had sent a car for us. This really was fancy!

We pushed our trolley over and said hello. The driver loaded our luggage into the boot of the hotel car, and we climbed into the coolness of the soft leather seats.

'Welcome to the Shangri-La Mactan,' he said. 'Please take a cool towel and some water, and enjoy your ride to the resort.'

What a way to start our first night away on our big adventure. It was a sign of good things to come, I was sure.

'Mummy, I love our year of travel!' Emmie said.

'It's not going to be like this all the time,' I said with a laugh. 'But we are so very lucky!'

As we drove towards the resort, we gazed out of the tinted windows at messy streets lined with small shacks made of metal cast-offs, and families obviously struggling to make a living. In the Philippines, more than one-fifth of the population lives below the poverty line, and many are unable to provide an education for their children. I was immediately hit with the contrast of our lives; it reaffirmed how fortunate we were to even dream of travelling like this, and that we were so, so lucky to have the ability to make it happen.

While we were going to a resort right now, for most of our time away we would be staying at guesthouses owned by locals, using local transport and contributing to the local economy. I still hadn't quite figured out how to help Emmie understand poverty, but I wanted her to know that many families face incredible hardships, yet continue every day with resilience and optimism. I wanted her to understand how she could support others in a way that was actually helpful and had a long-term impact.

We arrived at the resort after more than twelve hours of travelling, and checked into our gorgeous room. It was the first night of our trip, and I wish I could have bottled the air. I felt like joy was radiating from our bodies as we jumped around the room before falling asleep.

A few hours later, I was woken by a little face pressed into mine.

'Mummy, we are on our big adventure! Let's go to the pool.'

I had my priorities straight, though. 'Soon, Emmie, soon. Buffet breakfast first!'

We spent the day in pure happiness—along with disbelief that this was really, finally happening—swimming and playing in the pools and the ocean, and trying to rest, which was just about impossible with Emmie's energy.

The resort was just what we needed to start our trip, and it got even better when Emmie made a friend. Well, I think his mum made friends with me first. I was lying on a sun lounge, having excused myself from Emmie's intense pool-game schedule, when I felt a bump. I looked up to see an elegant lady perched at my feet.

'Hello,' she said, sticking out her hand and speaking in that rapid-fire way Hong Kong women do. 'I am Rajani. I saw you here and wanted to say hello. My son is six, and if he and your daughter play together, we will both get some time to ourselves. Can I offer you a drink?'

Rajani and her husband had hangovers from the night before, and while he was still in the room, she felt the best way to fix her problem was a swim and a wine. I loved her on sight.

Emmie and John, Rajani's son, played on the waterslides while we chatted on the lounges. Her husband wandered down, and we all played hide-and-seek on the beach, swam in the ocean, fed the tropical fish and relaxed.

We were having so much fun that on day two of our trip, I broke the budget—already! Day two!—and extended for one more night. We stayed with our new friends, watching the cultural show, eating suckling pig and drinking beer while Emmie and John joined the Filipino performers on stage for traditional games and dances, their nimble feet tapping between fast-moving bamboo poles.

The next day we were ready to go. As we were leaving our room, Emmie flew a little paper aeroplane onto the bulkhead above our bed. She had drawn a picture and a holiday message on the paper, and it's probably still there now, or maybe another family found this little travel love note on their adventures. I hope so.

The hotel car dropped us at the ferry terminal, and I felt like a bit of an impostor until it had driven away. I had my backpack on my back and my daughter by my side, and we stood in the queue to buy ferry tickets to the island of Bohol, about two hours from Cebu. Now our real adventure was beginning!

The port was dusty, dirty and gritty, the kind of place where buildings look almost finished yet simultaneously about to collapse. There was a mishmash of walls and fences, machinery and dusty roadways, and a metal maze for people to queue in as the dust swirled and the man at the one open window slowly sold tickets.

I loved it. This was what I'd been waiting for, to be out in the world with Emmie. And to be honest, I was feeling pretty cool with my backpack. Yep, nothing to see here, just a mum off to explore the world with her daughter by her side. I felt like I was going to burst out of my body.

We bought our tickets, labelled and dropped the backpack onto a trolley for loading into the ferry hull, and waited under a tin shed for boarding, playing Uno and sweating in the heat.

Things were going well, and we arrived in Bohol after a comfortable two-hour ride across the Cebu Strait.

Once our pack was carefully thrown out of the hull, I heaved it onto my back and off we clomped down the long concrete wharf in the sunshine. We negotiated a rate with a tricycle driver waiting outside the terminal and motored along to a small guesthouse up the hill from Panglao Beach that I'd booked the day before. I didn't like being locked in, and last-minute bookings were how we rolled, but this time I was lucky to get anything at all. It was peak season as well as the Chinese New Year holiday, and accommodation was expensive and scarce. I'd had no idea, and I made a mental note to check for holidays in the countries we were travelling to, which of course, I never did.

Our room at the guesthouse was on the ground floor of a family home. It had a double bed made up with sweet floral sheets, and a tiny ensuite. The host looked offended when I rolled out our sleeping sheets, and I felt bad, but I'd travelled with a sleeping sheet since my early backpacker days. It's simply a silk slip that hooks over a pillow and is used like a sleeping bag, so you don't have to touch the guesthouse or hostel sheets or pillow.

As it turned out, we rarely used our sleeping sheets after the first few weeks of our travels, although Emmie loved hers whenever I pulled it out. The standard of accommodation had improved so much since I first went backpacking and, although we were still budget, we were nowhere near the dodgy level I had hit back then with Jacqui. Those were the days, though. Remembering how vast the world seemed then makes me sad about the speed of development today. How much will be left undeveloped by the time Emmie is old enough to take off on a trip by herself? Where will the explorers go when everything has been discovered?

After setting up the room, I found Emmie with a bunch of Korean girls, eating the sticky chicken and rice they'd just made in the communal kitchen.

'Can you get the recipe, Mum?' she asked as she entertained the girls with her chatter.

'She is so cute!' they giggled to each other as they ate. I was so happy to see that the special bond I'd often felt with other backpackers in hostels and guesthouses still existed, and I loved watching Emmie interacting with other young travellers.

The next day, we hired a tricycle and set off to see the famous Bohol Chocolate Hills, spluttering along in our little machine and gazing out at the dusty streets, small colourful villages and golden fields. There's nothing quite like hooning along past rice paddies, jungles and villages while you're squashed in the front seat next to a driver using motorcycle handlebars to steer, with music blaring and rosary beads hanging from the rear-view mirror.

After climbing to the lookout to see the surprisingly green Chocolate Hills and spotting little furry tarsiers (possibly the cutest animals in the world, which I suspected were strategically placed so tourists could get the photos they'd come for), we arrived unexpectedly at the zipline. Releasing my fear and realising my strength in such an unexpected way was a huge moment for me so early in our trip, and it was all thanks to Emmie. I was learning just how much this little six year old could teach me.

After that emotional ride, I was happy for a little quiet time, so when our driver pulled into a reptile park for another unscheduled stop, I didn't argue. The park looked okay, and Emmie was desperate to see the snakes, so we paid our entry fee and wandered inside. It was a small park with a central shaded area surrounded by a circular walkway, grassy pens and large covered cages with giant snakes lying on cool concrete. Boxes of cold, colourful, scaly snakes were carefully being opened by one of the staff. These snakes were passed to the children to hold, while another staff member rotated them so they didn't get hot or distressed.

'Mum, watch this!' Emmie whispered as she held little snakes of all colours and sizes. She absolutely loved touching them, feeling them slide over her little hands. I'm not sure if we would do this now, as our opinion about interacting with wildlife has changed, but at the time it seemed like a good education for her.

As I sat there taking it all in, I noticed a woman who'd been staffing the little snack bar grab an old-fashioned boom box and microphone, and move near the snakes. She wore full make-up, a sparkling dress and a bouffant hairdo.

Wow, she's very glamorous for a snake expert, I thought, clueless and impressed.

'Hey Emmie, there's going to be a snake talk,' I yelled out to her. 'Come and grab a seat.'

Emmie wandered over holding a snake as the lady pressed play, put the microphone to her lips and struck a pose. Wait, what?

This wasn't a snake talk! Music blared out of the boom box, loud and distorted, while the woman mimed the song with exaggerated lips and gestures, and moved suggestively across the floor.

'Halloooooooooooooooooooooo!' Her mouth was wide open and she exaggeratedly wobbled her jaw and lips.

'What *is* this?' I screamed at Emmie, delighted and momentarily confused, as she stared at me with glee.

The most theatrical and unexpected Adele impersonation was now underway in this little roadside reptile park.

'Mum! Mum! She's a beautiful lady … but she is also a man!' Emmie yelled at me over the music, eyes dancing with delight.

We sat, entranced, as this shimmering lady mimed and cavorted around the park, simulating X-rated activities on a ladder as she climbed up to a wooden platform for the final note. We cheered our hearts out when the show ended. After the applause, the boom box was quickly packed away and she returned to her shop, where she sat preening and accepting praise from the guests.

What a way to end the day! It was just so very Philippines—loose, unplanned and not wrapped up in the rigidity we knew from home.

'Mummy, how can a lady be a lady and a man at the same time?' Emmie asked on the way home to the guesthouse. I could tell she had been thinking about it.

I've always answered Emmie honestly, and my only concern is explaining things correctly, especially when I'm not sure of the right language or sensitivities. We talked about how some people are born looking like a woman, but are a man in their heart, their feelings and on the inside—and vice versa—and how some people feel like both a boy and a girl, and some feel like neither. And how it should never matter; we are all just a bunch of imperfect people here on Earth trying to find happiness.

'Everyone is different, Emmie, and it's important to accept people for who they are. Just like we want people to accept us for who we are.'

'Travelling girls with dirty hair?'

'Ha ha, yep, that's it. Shower tonight, missy!'

And then it was on with life. Kids are so awesome.

We decided to go snorkelling the next day and booked a trip out to tiny Balicasag Island on a Filipino *banca*, a traditional boat that looks like a large canoe with outriggers and a canopy over the top. We packed up my daypack with our snorkels, masks, sarongs, sunscreen, camera and GoPro, and set off in the early light, holding hands and wandering down the hill to meet a bloke and his boat.

Is that strange? You have to have faith when you're travelling. If your guesthouse arranges for you to meet a man and his boat at 6.00 am, you just trust that it's okay. We didn't go out late at night, we didn't put ourselves into risky situations, but we did trust the locals we met and stayed with.

Our man was waiting on the sand for us in the golden morning light. I paid him the day rate, and he pointed out our boat waiting just offshore. It was low tide, so we waded out through ankle-deep water past hundreds of pink-spotted starfish lying in the shallows. With each step, we saw more dotted around us as we picked our way towards the tiny boat.

'Forty-nine, 50, 51 ...' Emmie counted the starfish as she tiptoed past them, getting closer to the rising sun and our little *banca*. We said hello to the captain, climbed aboard and set off across the Bohol Sea.

I sat on the side of the boat with my arm around Emmie, who snuggled into me as we sailed out from the shallows. The sun rose above the deep blue water, and shone down on us, and the ocean splashed little salty drops over our arms and legs. To describe this as happiness would be right, but the pure joy I felt at this very moment was so much more.

'We did it, Emmie,' I said, my heart full.

'Yeah, Mum, I love you. I'm so happy.' She gave me a hug and we sat together, peaceful in the sunshine.

It had only taken us a few days to start living a super happy life. That's all anyone wants, right? If you drill down to the very core? We just want to be happy. I thought back to everything we'd left behind—the expensive clothes and toys, the house, the stuff. None of it had ever filled my heart with this much happiness and contentment. I had everything I needed right here—and I never wanted this feeling to end.

We arrived at Balicasag Island, and pulled up on the white sand. After paying our visitors' fee, we were approached by a guide who wanted to take us out snorkelling on the reef. He didn't speak much English and I didn't speak Tagalog, but we agreed to a price and he motioned for me to get in his tiny canoe, a big happy grin on his face. I looked at the canoe—it was pretty small. Couldn't I just swim out to the reef? It wasn't that far. I grabbed our GoPro and started walking into the water, but the man stopped me.

'No, no, lady,' he said, shaking his head and pointing to the canoe. I'd paid the money, so I was getting the canoe ride, whether I wanted it or not.

'Seriously, I don't think this is a good idea. I think I may capsize your canoe,' I told him, laughing and miming me falling out of the canoe. I am pretty sure he knew what I meant, but he shrugged and laughed along with me.

Fine. Grunting and groaning, and with Emmie giggling, I wobbled and teetered and folded myself into the canoe, and off we paddled to the reef.

'Hey Mum, don't fall out,' Emmie laughed, as she rocked the canoe from side to side.

'Oh, ha ha, Emmie. If I go down, we all go down! Don't risk it!'

We were relatively stable and upright until we stopped above the reef. Then I realised that I hadn't anticipated how truly difficult extracting myself was going to be. Oh my God, how on earth was I supposed to get out?

If you have ever shoved a chubby bikini-clad body into a very small canoe, you will know how unstable it is when you're trying to stand, especially if you have to hoist yourself up, keeping everything intact. It's no simple task to keep your balance, stand up and navigate your way into the water. With every tiny movement, I felt the canoe lurch from side to side.

'I am not sure this is a good idea,' I said to the man, but his gestures and smile told me it was all good, to just do my best and get out of the canoe. But I couldn't, I was sure it was going to tip over.

'Emmie, what am I going to do?' I whined, laughing but desperate. She was laughing back at me, absolutely delighted at my predicament, and I hammed it up a little for her.

'Just jump in Mum, it's easy!' she said, and she jumped in from the canoe, like the little show-off she is. She slid her mask on, popped her snorkel in her mouth and paddled around. 'Come on, it's beautiful down there!'

With amused resignation, I realised that I was going to have to do it. I had no choice. Heaving myself up, I tried to gracefully manoeuvre overboard but, instead, I catapulted off the edge of the canoe and smashed into the water. My feet pushed off the side and sent the canoe flying out behind me. The guide's snorkel gear flew off into the sea as the canoe lurched over and started sinking.

'I'm so sorry!' I yelled out as I thought to myself, *I bloody told you so!*

The guide laughed and collected his stuff from the water, and a friend came to help him drag his canoe to shore and empty it.

Emmie and I popped our heads below the surface, and under the sparkling sun and blue Philippines skies, we snorkelled over delicate patterns of colourful corals surrounded by fish. Little

Nemo clownfish poked their heads out of their anemone homes to frighten us off, and golden bubbles rose to the surface like tiny stars. We reached a spectacular drop-off where we spotted turtles cruising past, and for the next hour we floated, paddled and swam.

Our next stop was the Virgin Island sandbar, a white slash of sand surrounded by blue water. Locals had set up little coconut stalls and were cooking seafood on huge metal plates as we pulled up alongside other blue and white painted *bancas*. We grabbed a coconut each and wandered around the island, spotting starfish and splashing in the water until we saw our captain hurrying towards us.

'We must go,' he said. 'There's a big storm coming. Hurry.' He pointed in the direction we'd sailed from.

'Um, Mum, why are we going to sail into the storm?' asked Emmie.

I wasn't sure. It didn't really make sense to get into our tiny boat and sail off towards the angry black clouds, but we climbed in and set off back to base. It started out just a little choppy, but as we sailed on, the waves turned from blue to dark grey and grew higher and wilder. I grabbed Emmie, pulling her close to me and holding on as the waves crashed in over the boat. Thankfully, we were going straight into them rather than being hit from the side, but I felt like we were on the S.S. *Minnow* and I held onto Emmie and hoped this boat was strong and our captain capable. We were flying up and slamming down as the black clouds stormed overhead and rain hammered down on us.

'Mum! What will you save, your camera or me?' yelled Emmie over the sound of the storm. She slipped off her seat onto the floor, and I pulled her up and held her tightly as the boat lurched through the water. 'Mummy, will we be okay?' She clutched my arm.

'We'll be fine, baby. We are good swimmers, and I've got you. Nothing is going to happen to the boat anyway, it's just a little storm.'

The captain was straining to hold the rudder, and the motor was being flung out of the water as we burst over each crest and slammed down. We held on as I tried to make Emmie laugh, and then, finally, we were through the storm, exhausted, saturated and thankful.

Slowly, the no-longer-nervous-looking captain navigated his way close to shore and we splashed into waist-deep water, me holding my surprisingly still-dry bag with camera high above my head as we battled our way in.

'That was fun!' said Emmie, and we laughed as the sun peeked through the black clouds. But mine was a nervous laugh. That was a bit of a scare …

That night, I thought about our day—the beautiful sunrise, the starfish, the snorkelling, the canoe fiasco, the sandbar with locals and fresh coconuts, and the *banca* ride through the storm. If we were at home in Sydney, what would I have been doing? I would have left for work, saying a quick goodbye to Emmie, spent over an hour on the train and the day at my desk in the city while Emmie was at her desk at school. I would have spent another hour and a half getting home late, just in time to put Emmie to bed. The difference was staggering. For so long we'd been trapped inside while this amazing world was outside, waiting for us. I was so relieved we were here.

A few days later, we took two ferries and hopped over to the mystical island of Siquijor, avoided by many Filipinos because of its reputation for witchcraft. I really wanted to see a witchdoctor, known as a Bolo Bolo healer, and I asked at the front desk of our hotel if they knew where I could visit one.

'I am sorry, but Bolo Bolo man is building a home in the mountains and his mobile phone is out of range,' they told me.

'Good,' said Emmie. She wanted no part of it.

Picturing this mystical healer cutting timber in denim jeans with a Nokia 2110 strapped to his waistband kind of took the intrigue out of it anyway.

We both needed a healer, though. A weird fungus infection had started growing on Emmie's face, and continued to spread even after she'd taken the course of emergency antibiotics I'd brought from home. My ear had started aching, so I'd started on the adult antibiotics. When I ran out, we wandered down the dirt road outside the hotel to a tiny wooden shack that stocked medicine and bought more for a few dollars. No prescription needed. Everything was available. We paid by the pill.

We were in bliss on the beach at Siquijor. We snorkelled over the coral and fish-filled reefs, swung on hammocks and made mandalas in the sand. We roamed around on tricycles with locals who showed us lookouts, rivers and beaches with white sand and blue water. We hiked into the jungle and jumped from the milky green Cambugahay Falls, which cascaded over the rocks framed by banana leaves and palms, and swung out on rope swings, landing in the middle of blue-green pools. Emmie made a friend, Felicia from France, and they played all day without a common language, using smiles, gestures and the language of kids to get along.

Even though we were on a protected reef, it was sad to see many guests not respecting the environment, walking all over the corals when the tide was out and taking marine life from the little ocean pools. It upset us, and when a man brought a starfish up to the swimming pool for his small daughter to play with, Emmie decided to take action.

'Excuse me, but starfish belong in the ocean,' she said. 'Can I take it back to its home please?' And she did.

Go Emmie.

Even though my ear hurt, I played Emmie's pool games against my better judgment, diving down to get our toys from the bottom, playing Marco Polo and doing whatever she wanted me to. Emmie's fungus was not improving, either. It was only the second week on our trip, but both of us were getting into a bit of trouble.

CHAPTER 5

Superwomen on a waterfall

We set off on the ferry again, over to the port at Dumaguete, playing Uno until Emmie's cheating got so bad I ended the game.

'That's it Emmie! Game over. I'm not playing when you cheat every time.'

I packed the cards away, annoyed that we couldn't just play a fun game together. I knew that she was only six, but there had to be a limit!

Cheating at Uno was Emmie's little weakness (and the more she saw it annoyed me, the more she did it), but we both had our things to work on. I rarely lost my temper but when I did, I got angry. Emmie knew she could get me to breaking point, and she did it with an infuriating smirk and defiance in her eyes. I promised myself to count to ten, twenty, one hundred … but I usually only got to four or so before I cracked.

In Dumaguete, the locals helped us find the jetty where a small boat would take us back to Cebu. It all seemed so easy. Having more than a couple of weeks to travel, explore and relax meant there was literally no holiday stress. We didn't have a deadline. We could turn up whenever and wherever, and if something went wrong it didn't bother us, because we had time to sort it out. If we loved where we were, we could always stay longer, and if we didn't, we simply travelled on.

That kind of flexibility—of time, of choice—is a luxury we generally don't give ourselves in everyday life. At home, we are always locking ourselves in. Loans, jobs, mortgages, rental contracts, timetables, kids' sport, shopping, bills—it's a life built on deadlines and routine that becomes more rigid and inflexible with every new commitment and responsibility we add. I think we need to give ourselves more freedom. Life is so much more than a checklist of jobs to be ticked off. We need time to explore, to let life happen and to see where we end up. Just let yourself go … see what happens.

When we got off the little boat at a jetty in Cebu, we found the bus to Oslob, climbed on, told the driver where we were staying and trusted that he knew where to let us off. He did, dropping us right near Langnason's Place, a little guesthouse I'd found online the day before. It was down a dirt track off the main road and backed onto a rough and rocky ocean. Pretty and clean, it had a swimming pool and common kitchen, and most importantly it was owned by a local family, so there were kids for Emmie to play with and we were supporting the community by staying there. The owner, Marilou, ran the guesthouse while her husband worked away for most of the year on cargo ships. This year-old venture was their gamble in earning enough money to get him back permanently to the Philippines. Marilou's sister Melba worked alongside her, while their younger sister Melanie was a nurse at the local clinic. The patriarch of the family, who we also called Papa, had a shiny black car for taking guests on excursions and was doted on by the family.

We'd come to Oslob to swim with the whale sharks and visit more of Cebu's stunning waterfalls. I was uneasy about the whale sharks, but since we were nearby I felt like we should take the opportunity. I knew that *Lonely Planet* ignored Oslob as a destination because of its whale shark tourism, but I'd also heard that the industry supported the town and was well managed.

Emmie and I talked it over, and she wasn't sure if she wanted to do it, either. We decided to give it a go, although I may have pushed Emmie into it. Looking back, I think I just selfishly wanted to swim with the whale sharks, no matter what.

We set off early in the morning, both nervous and a little reluctant. I had a feeling in my belly that I was doing something I shouldn't, but when we arrived at the beachfront it seemed really well organised, if crowded. We had a short induction, were given life jackets and jumped into a *banca* with about ten other tourists. My ear was still sore and I'd lost my earplug, so I had shoved a plasticine concoction in and hoped it wouldn't leak.

We were rowed out about 50 metres from shore and told to float around just in front of the *banca*. The whale sharks would swim past, and we would get a chance to see them and get photos, of course. Everyone wanted photos.

'Mummy, I'm scared,' Emmie said quietly, a little overwhelmed by the churning water, the myriad boats, the whistles and yelling.

'You'll be fine,' I told her, not really believing she was nervous; she loved snorkelling. But I was a bit hesitant, too. 'You're the best little snorkeller I know, and we'll swim together. We'll be alright.'

While it all looked organised from shore, it was anything but in the water. I kept a hold of Emmie's arm as we jumped in together, and she was fine until a woman jumped in on top of her in a panic. She knocked Emmie's snorkel and mask from her face while floundering around in the water, screaming for her partner, who also didn't know how to swim. They floated off together, arms and legs flapping in the air, leaving a scared little Emmie in their wake.

I was furious, and I felt so bad for Emmie. I held her up and tried to get her mask back on while the boat manoeuvred around us. The outrigger went up and smashed down into the waves, narrowly missing our heads, then the plasticine fell out of my ear and the disgusting, meaty water rushed in.

Small whale sharks swam nearby, eating the chump that had attracted them in, and as they lurched around for bait in the murky water, they looked nothing at all like the majestic creatures I'd pictured. Tourists swam in front and around them, getting too close and posing for photos with their friends and their selfie sticks. It all felt sad and unnatural, and I was annoyed at myself for going against my gut and bringing us here.

I thought back to 1997 when I was backpacking with Jacqui and we'd jumped on a small fishing boat to the Perhentian Islands in Malaysia. Out on the ocean, the crew had started yelling and jumping in excitement, pointing to a giant whale shark that had surfaced right next to our little boat. I had been so freaked out that I hadn't appreciated how incredible that moment was. I wish I had. This was nothing like it.

We climbed out, dried off and met Papa. I felt like I'd let Emmie down by encouraging her to swim with the whale sharks when she really didn't want to, and I felt bad for the whale sharks. I'd definitely made the wrong decision.

Luckily, our next stop was the incredible five-tiered Aguinid Falls to wash the dirty feeling away. Papa had made a big deal about how he had carefully chosen these falls for us, but then laughed and revealed that, as there hadn't been any rain for a while, they were the only ones flowing.

As we wandered to the ramshackle wooden ticket office at the base of the mountain, two local ladies in t-shirts, shorts and thongs said hello and walked beside us.

'You want a guide?' they asked me. 'Very difficult to climb waterfall, you need a guide for the baby.'

'Yes, of course,' I replied with a smile. 'How much is it?' And for $5 each, we were climbing the falls with two lovely locals.

It turned out to be the best $10 I'd ever spent. This was *not* just a nice little stroll to a milky aqua waterfall with a picturesque swing and swimming hole. This was a full-on workout, climbing all five tiers of the towering falls, up smooth silver rock walls that, while steep, weren't slippery—apparently due to the water's high mineral content. We were surrounded by rainforest and dressed only in our swimming costumes and hiking sandals as our lovely guides helped us up the falls.

They more than helped me. These superwomen pulled and pushed me up the side of the waterfall as I grabbed little handholes and heaved myself up onto each ledge. The women were tiny and nimble. And wearing thongs. And they were having a good laugh at me, as was I—we were all laughing. It was so much fun.

'Come on, Mum, you can do it,' yelled Emmie, always encouraging me through her laughter.

'Yes, come on, mama Evie,' the ladies laughed along.

Water flowed all over us as we climbed up and over and into each stage of the falls, rock jumping and swimming in the clear blue pools. We glided down natural rock slides and swam into a hidden cave behind a curtain of water. We were alone in this gorgeous nature, and we adored the two women who'd helped us get there.

But the side of my head was starting to hurt from my earache, and I was getting worried. My body was making it clear that it'd had enough. It was time to go.

We made our way down to Papa and began the drive back to the guesthouse. My ear was pounding, and it felt like every little bump in the road was making it worse. I had to see a doctor, so Papa dropped us off at the small district hospital in town.

The hospital was a simple white building with open doors and windows, and young Filipino nurses milling around in starched white uniforms. I was assessed and we waited our turn in the queue, sitting on little chairs in a waiting room with the well-groomed nurses looking on.

'Are you going to be okay, Mummy?' Emmie was worried. 'Would it help if we played a game?'

'I'm sorry, ladybug. I can't play a game because my ear is so sore, but you can play on my phone if you like.' I needed to lie down, and I needed to stop the pain.

After a short wait, we were called in to see the doctor, who asked if he could take a look inside my ear—and used his iPhone torch to do it. Far out. It worried me; could he see what he needed to with an iPhone? I was sure he was a good doctor, and it was an indication of what equipment was lacking rather than his ability, but it stressed me out. Still, I gleefully accepted a pain injection and a prescription for a bunch of drugs that we grabbed from the chemist before returning to the guesthouse. Then I lay down in bed and slept for twelve hours while Emmie watched *Pitch Perfect* over and over again on the computer.

The next day, my ear started weeping fluid, and the right side of my face, jaw and neck was so swollen I couldn't close my mouth. I was a little worried, although it was a hazy worry with the drugs and the sleeping. Emmie sat by me and stroked my hair, watched the iPad or played with the kids at the guesthouse. If I had to be sick, I was glad it was here where we had such a kind family to look after us.

I emailed my travel insurance company, and a nurse called and recommended that I see a specialist at the university in Cebu City. My sister also went to her local doctor in Sydney and had him call to talk me through what I should be doing and taking. Everyone agreed that I had the right medicine but should also see the specialist. The insurance company made an appointment for me, and the next day Papa drove us into the city, a few hours north of Oslob. We made an important stop to buy Emmie a helium balloon from a street seller and then found the specialist's rooms at the university. He confirmed that my eardrum was more than 40 per cent perforated and wanted to stick an old contraption in to suck out the moisture. I quickly declined—it looked scary, and I was now feeling very protective of my poor ear.

'You cannot get your ear wet for six weeks,' the doctor told me. 'But the good news is, since your eardrum has already burst, you can fly.'

That *was* good news. Since I couldn't swim or get my ear wet at all we would probably move on to somewhere cooler, but we would stay at Langnason's Place until I was better.

Three weeks into our trip and I had a burst eardrum, and Emmie had a fungus face. This wasn't quite what I'd been expecting.

I returned to the local doctor for more drugs and painkillers, and, eventually, I was up and about. I watched Emmie swim in the pool and threw the pool toys for her to fetch from the bottom. I had careful showers and left my hair dirty, not risking even one drop getting close to my ear. I drank cup after cup of tea with packet creamer, and slowly felt better—and just in time for my birthday! The Langnason family brought me a creamy sponge cake and sang 'Happy Birthday' as Marilou turned on the ever-present karaoke machine.

I love karaoke. I love picking the songs, punching the numbers in, waiting for my turn and singing away, pretending I'm a star. I just love it all except I've always felt uncomfortable with the performance part of it. In Australia, when you take the microphone everyone watches, and you have to add dance moves, fill the musical interludes and put on a show. Not in the Philippines! Karaoke is such a way of life, it's just one part of a get-together, a lunch or evening drinks; even families have small machines in their loungerooms. The Langnasons' songbooks were huge and filled with music from all decades, countries and genres. There were nursery rhymes for the kids and hymns for the pious. There was something for everyone.

When the machine was fired up, life went on as normal and conversations continued as the song numbers were punched in. There was no standing in front of the group. People sat in their seats and belted their hearts out before putting the microphone down and continuing their conversation, dinner or drink. And then someone else had a go. It was very casual.

'Marilou, I love this karaoke!' I said as another guest sang at the table while everyone ignored him.

'Evie, it's normal! Everyone has karaoke in the Philippines,' she said. 'Especially on Saturdays and Sundays, when people have finished work for the week, and can buy beer. They all get together and drink and sing.'

It was my birthday and I had to perform, even though no one had asked me to. I selected Fleetwood Mac, and I stood up and sang my heart out, adding a little shuffle while no one watched. Emmie got up and belted out a Miley Cyrus song as I cheered her on, then we wandered off to bed feeling content. Happy birthday to me.

I may have been in bed for a few days, but that didn't mean we missed learning about where we were. On a trip to the doctor for a check-up, Marilou took us to the stunning Our Lady of the Immaculate Conception church where we watched a mass wedding for couples who couldn't afford their own ceremonies. Hundreds of young men and women in borrowed suits and dazzlingly white bridal gowns paraded outside and filed into the church, each emerging joyfully together as husband and wife. Mass happiness was beautiful to see.

We were in a land of more than 7500 stunning tropical islands and I was unable to swim, so it was best to go—for now. I was well enough to move on, so we searched Skyscanner for cheap flights to anywhere, preferably somewhere cool. We found tickets to Taiwan for the next day, booked them, reloaded the backpack and got ready to set off again. Sadly, this meant that we wouldn't get to spend months wandering through the Philippines as I'd hoped, but we had somewhere new to explore. We farewelled our Filipino family, and they sat on the side of the road with us, waiting for the local bus to Cebu City.

Before we left, Emmie and I had given the young girl who worked at the guesthouse some money for her family. She'd looked after Emmie while I was sick and had told us her story. Her family lived five hours away from Oslob, and on her one day off work each week she travelled home on the bus to take them the money she had earned. I will always remember how happy she was when we passed it to her, how her face lit up and then was filled with tears, and how I felt in that moment. I'm not sharing this to make out that we're something special, or that we have money to throw around, but jeez, we're not all given an even crack at life, are we? It's just luck that I popped out in Sydney, Australia, to a middle-class family who could provide my sister and me with everything we needed. I've worked hard all my life, so Emmie is also fortunate that I can give her opportunities, too. Many people have more than us, but many, many have less. I think it's so important that Emmie is mindful of that, and we try to be generous where we can.

'It feels good to be kind, doesn't it?' I said to Emmie, and she agreed with a huge smile. When she gives people food or help, she feels happy and I know she has learned that the joy of giving lasts longer and feels so much better than receiving. I mean, she's still a greedy little kid (just like I'm a greedy adult), no questions there, but she loves giving, too, and that's important.

Papa and the family hailed the city bus for us from the side of the road, and we climbed on. Emmie snuggled down on my lap to sleep, and I half-watched a James Bond movie playing on the

TV screen above the driver as we flashed past palm trees, wild coastline and dusty villages. A few hours later we entered the chaos of Cebu City and were spewed out into the grubby, gravelly bus station.

CHAPTER 6

Farewell, fungus face

After a three-hour flight, we landed in Taipei with minds and hearts open to this unfamiliar city. We knew little about Taiwan, and this added an extra layer of adventure for us. Arriving into a country I'd never thought of visiting until hours before was like waiting for a party to start—there was so much anticipation, and I wasn't sure what was ahead for us, but I knew it was going to be fun.

We jumped on the bus to the city, zooming down the freeway in the blackness of early morning. I promised myself that I would take everything in, keep my eyes open and alert, and absorb it all. The unknowing had me so eager to explore.

The feeling of freedom and happiness was strong, but so was Emmie's face fungus. We hadn't managed to completely kill it, so she'd started another course of antibiotics before we left the Philippines. The medicine didn't seem to be working, though, and I worried about her taking so much of it with little result. The angry red scabs had come back under her nose, and a few patches had appeared high on her cheeks. While it didn't seem to bother her, I knew it couldn't be good, and I was hoping the cooler weather would help it clear.

I'd booked us into the Rido Hotel in a suburb called Da'an Park. It seemed central and, without knowing anything about the city, I'd taken a punt. It was close to a good train line and, most importantly, the original Din Tai Fung, the restaurant famous for its *xiao long bao*, those delicious dumplings filled with pork and soup. The hotel was golden, gaudy and glamorous, with a glass elevator, frescos on the walls and mirrors on the bedroom ceiling. Our room was furnished in heavy dark wood with thick copper and burgundy fabrics and a luxurious daybed that overlooked the park. The staff sent us cookies and sweets for Emmie and gave us umbrellas for the rain. We loved it.

We set off that afternoon to explore, wearing almost all of our clothes for warmth. We were travelling with only summer gear, and it was raining and a cool 16 degrees in the city. We stayed undercover, visiting the Taipei Museum of Contemporary Art and the Toy Museum, easily finding our way on Taipei's impressive metro. Honestly, if a city has a good public transport system, exploring is so easy. Taipei not only had an easy metro, but the trains arrived to music; there were breastfeeding rooms, the cleanest station toilets we'd ever seen and huge artworks covering the walls of the underground walkways. We didn't know the language and we were completely unprepared, but the Taiwanese people were so kind. They would stand for us on the trains and ask if we needed help. They were always smiling and saying hello, and were patient as we bumbled our way along.

That night, we ventured out to Din Tai Fung to satisfy my soup-dumpling obsession. There was a crowd three- or four-people deep waiting for tables or holding up white cards filled with their takeaway orders. Years after first tasting *xiao long bao* at Din Tai Fung in Singapore with Jacqui, I was now at the dumpling homeland. When we finally got a table, my challenge was to get Emmie to try something other than rice. With her arms crossed, she stubbornly refused even a nibble.

'Emmie, this is my most favourite food. Please, will you try it? Just a little. I promise you'll like it,' I begged.

'Muuummm, I don't want to, it looks funny,' she said but, to my surprise, I eventually persuaded her. She frowned at me as she poked a dumpling, watched as the soup escaped into her spoon, and stuck her tongue out to taste a tiny drop.

'Mum, it's so good!' She slurped the soup and devoured the dumpling, then finished off the other four in the bamboo steamer. 'Can we order some more?'

She ate twelve more dumplings that night and a plate of green beans and pork. I was so proud that she'd tried something different—and we now had a common food obsession! Emmie's *xiao long bao* passion had begun, and for the rest of our travels, we hunted down Din Tai Fung restaurants wherever we were in the world.

Emmie went to the bathroom and came back laughing. 'Mum, you have to try the toilet!' she said, grabbing my arm and trying to pull me over to it. 'It plays running water sounds so no one can hear you wee—and you can wash your bum!' Din Tai Fung was a winner.

Emmie had been a star through our first month of travelling, and I was so impressed with how she was thriving on the road. She was willing to do anything—hiking, snorkelling, swimming, setting out on that *banca* through the waves—and she took our last-minute move to Taipei in her stride. She was loving the lack of structure and our loose way of doing things.

But as we finally, properly, started the schoolwork we had been given by Distance Education, I discovered that Emmie's adventurous side was the yin to her stubborn yang. I opened the blue folders that held the schoolwork and stared at hundreds of photocopied pages: it seemed to need a lot of planning. This wasn't good. I was expecting it to be easy and organised for me!

I'm not very structured, and while I like to travel without locking us into things, part of the reason is that I don't like planning. I don't care enough about it, and I just don't have the time as a solo parent. I also believe the magic happens when you stumble onto things. That said, I am a stickler for punctuality—when I remember to turn up.

'Okay, Emmie, just wait a sec and I'll get the work ready,' I said in my teacher voice, faking confidence as she sat at the table. Finally, I had it all together and set down some maths for us to do.

'Right. So, all we need to do now is practise some counting by twos. It will be easy, and then we can fill in the worksheet and we're done! We can go outside and explore.'

She looked away. She was having none of it.

'Okay, so let's count by twos, Emmie. Can you start?'

She looked at me in defiance. 'Six, three, one … '

'Oh, ha ha, Emmie. Come on, let's get this right. I'll start with two! What comes after two?'

'Six.'

This was not what I had imagined. Was this what schoolwork was going to be like every time? We couldn't even do the most basic lesson. I could feel myself deflating. I should have prepared more. I pulled out the coloured counters and arranged them into twos.

'Come on, honey, look at the counters and let's get this done! I know you know how to count by twos, let's do it together and then we can go out exploring. I can't wait!' My grin was maniacal, and my voice inflected hard with fake positivity and desperation.

'Five.'

Nothing before or since has had the ability to make me leap from zero to fuse blown, steam pouring out of my ears and scary devil voice rising. Trying to teach Emmie was a punishment coupled with confusion. I just didn't understand why she wouldn't do it. I knew she tried to impress her teachers at home and did what they asked, so why couldn't she do that for me? And even though I knew she wasn't a desk-learner, I needed her to get the work done so we could get outside. It was only 30 minutes of pain for a whole day of fun. *Arggghhh.*

Unfortunately, this was exactly how it would continue. Emmie would sit with a determined look on her face, not caring that I was having a breakdown. She was only open to learning when she decided it would benefit her, and not before. If there was reading to complete, she would ignore me or purposely say the wrong words. If there was maths, she would spew random numbers. I became a frustrated, angry demon, yelling and crying and begging her to please help me and do her work.

We occasionally managed to make it work if we were outside and used sticks and shells for counting, and when she didn't realise she was learning, but I had printed work and performance sheets that needed to be completed and sent back to school. I felt like an absolute failure.

Worse, when set up on the weekly online Zoom classroom with Mr Brown, her lovely 'real' teacher from Distance Education, she was the perfect student.

'Hello, Emmie! How are you and where are you today?' Mr Brown's happy voice would boom out of the laptop as he waved to her, and she would be a model student, completing her tasks with ease, behaving politely and whizzing through her work while giving me a sneaky smirk.

Poor Mr Brown. He tried so hard and was such a lovely support. He helped me get through the school year without losing my mind, and he sent Emmie a Christmas present. But I couldn't get the work to him when it just wasn't getting done consistently, even after he extended the deadlines. We did what we could when we could, and it was always a struggle. Eventually, I kind of gave up. Emmie's strategies to avoid schoolwork were usually successful, and off we'd go exploring—as we did in Taipei. This was what I considered to be her real education anyway. We practised maths and reading and learned history, geography and religion as we wandered, and I felt that she was learning more through travel than she would sitting at a desk.

We abandoned school that day, as we would so many more times, and made our way to the Chiang Kai-shek Memorial Hall for the changing of the guards. I felt my shoulders sag and my eyes roll back in my head when Emmie spotted, of all things, a *Frozen* exhibition in the forecourt. Here we were, exploring a new country, and I had a child hanging off me, begging for Disney. Oh, the lessons we are sent! I wanted to say no. I wanted to say that I would have let her if she had done her schoolwork, and that we were there to learn about Taiwan, not to top-up on *Frozen*. But then I thought, *why not?* Why shouldn't she see something that was going to make her happy? Restriction and routine was part of our old life. We could do whatever we wanted, so we did.

'Sure, Emmie,' I said. 'Let's go.'

'What, Mum, really?' She was surprised that I'd agreed and so thrilled, I think only partly for seeing *Frozen* but mostly because I'd listened to her and she felt she was driving this bus, too. It was important for Emmie to know that she had a voice in this trip, for me to respect what she wanted to do and really listen to her. We were in this together, school or no school.

Off we went to the entrance, where we discovered that there was a −10-degree ice world inside and we had to suit up in puffy onesies to protect ourselves against the cold. We wandered past gigantic ice sculptures, played in the snow and bobsledded down a huge ice slide, screaming and crashing into the safety mats at the bottom. It was a different Taipei experience than I'd expected, but that was what made it great. And it was Emmie's choice.

We still had time to see the changing of the guards and wander around the gardens, smelling the delicate pink cherry blossoms that had begun to flower and buying fish food by putting coins into the mouth of an orange ceramic koi, with pretty little bags of food dropping out of his belly.

Taipei taught us a lot. We discovered our openness to self-selecting religion here, if you can call it religion. Maybe it's more about a way of doing things, a way of believing that is flexible and open. I had been brought up in a slightly religious family, and I'd enjoyed mass when Emmie started Catholic kindergarten, especially the feeling of community and support, and hearing the kids sing always made me teary. But I suppose for Emmie and me, religion, or spirituality, was becoming more about how we wanted to live and the values we felt were important, like acceptance, kindness, a connection to nature and a sense of community.

In the evening, Emmie and I made our way in drizzling rain to the revered Mengjia Longshan Temple, through the crowds all softly passing by, bumping colourful umbrellas under sparkling lights. Locals patiently waited in long, snaking queues for street vendors' big metal tins of doughy buns to finish steaming, and we inhaled the meaty scent of pork and sausage and the occasional whiff of the Taiwanese favourite, the infamous stinky tofu.

The temple courtyard was colourful and bright, decorated with glowing lanterns and monkey and deity figurines to celebrate the Chinese New Year and the start of the Year of the Monkey. A small line of people waited to walk under the lanterns for good luck. Emmie is all about good luck, so we joined in and then wandered around the courtyard. Entering the ancient temple, we immediately felt a calmness and sense of peace as around us worshippers prayed, lit candles and incense, and monks softly chanted and gave out blessings. We sucked in the sweet scent of the incense as we watched it curl upwards in smoky waves from three huge golden urns. We were ready to pay our respects, but weren't really sure what to do.

'Maybe we can figure it out, Emmie,' I whispered. Then, through luck or divine intervention, a young man in a suit stopped in front of us.

'Hello, do you need help?' he asked through the soft chanting.

'Oh, yes please. We'd love to pray but we're not sure what to do,' I answered.

'Can you help us please?' asked Emmie.

'Of course!' he said with a smile. 'Everyone is welcome to pray here. Let me show you.'

Together, we lit three sticks of incense each and stood before the altar. Raising the incense to our foreheads, we bowed three times and then turned and bowed to the sky. We introduced ourselves to the gods, telling them who we were and where we were from. Emmie was taking a while; the gods were apparently getting a very detailed story.

'Mum, shhhhh, I'm making friends with the gods,' she hissed at me when I tried to move her along.

We said a prayer of thanks and then placed one incense stick into each golden urn, where they stuck up in the sand and sent a smoky trail skywards as we breathed in the scent, the goodness and the beautiful vibe. The feeling was so strong, I was almost in tears as I listened to the hymns and chanting and let the atmosphere of love and kindness wrap around me like a blanket.

Emmie noticed people shaking crescent-shaped blocks of wood with chipped red paint and dropping them onto the carpet.

'Excuse me, what are they doing?' she asked the man who was helping us.

'This is Bwa-Bwei, where we ask the gods for guidance,' he said. 'You can ask the gods a question, and you will see the answer in the wood. If both moons land with the curved part up, it is no. If both smooth parts are up, it is no. But if you have one of each side, your answer is yes.'

'I want to do it,' she said, taking two crescents and holding them in her hands.

'Make your wish,' we told her as she dropped the crescents to the ground. They clattered on the worn carpet and stopped.

It was one of each.

'Yes! Hooray, Emmie, you got a yes! What did you wish for?'
I asked her.

'Mummy, guess what? I wished for the drought in Australia to
be over. It's going to come true!'

'That's a lovely wish for the Australian farmers, Emmie, well
done,' I said.

Before we left Longshan, there was one more ritual to explore.
We took a long container filled with thin wooden sticks and slowly
shook it until one fell out. There was a number at the end of the
stick, and we took it to a gentleman at a counter who gave us a
piece of paper, our fortune printed on it. The fortune could be
good or bad, but you're not stuck with it. If you don't like it, you
can leave it behind. If it's good, you take it with you and trust that
it will come to you. Our fortunes were good, our new friend told
us—travel, good health and adventures were ahead. We were
happy, and I slipped the paper into my bag.

Longshan set us on our way to loving Buddhism and its
foundation in kindness. We loved the rituals of prayer and Bwa-
Bwei, and while we might not have performed it all correctly, we
did our best and it was a beautiful experience.

'Mum, how can there be different religions?' Emmie asked as
we left, a little confused.

'Well, Emmie, let me think,' I said, trying to articulate how I
felt. 'Religion is kind of the name for something you believe in, like
God, or the power of the universe or the earth and nature, or
Buddha. There are lots of different religions, and some of them
have lots of gods, but they mostly believe in the same things, like
being kind to one another.'

'I like Buddhism,' she said, thinking out loud. 'I also love nature and animals and the universe. Can I take some from each and be a Nature Buddhist?'

'I don't see why not. I guess you're a Nature Buddhist. I'm joining, too!'

We felt this sense of calm and contentment the whole time we were in Taiwan. We climbed Elephant Mountain in thongs and gazed out over the city and Taipei 101, the tallest building in Taiwan, where we watched the sun set later that evening. We ate Taiwanese pork burgers called *guabao* and thousand-layer scallion cakes from street stalls, and we sniffed but never tried the stinky tofu. We visited galleries and museums, the flower markets and the hot springs in Beitou, where Emmie threw our waterproof camera into a spa, thinking the housing was closed. It wasn't. Bye bye camera. We rode buses and trains and ate our fill of *xiao long bao*. Then we decided to take the train down to Sun Moon Lake, a few hours south of Taipei, for a bit more exploring, stopping at Hualien on the way, to hike Taroko Gorge.

My ear was feeling so much better now, but I was still worried about Emmie's face, so I asked the guesthouse for a doctor. They gave us directions written in Mandarin and we wandered the streets with people directing us to a small lane with nondescript little doorways. Behind one of them was the clinic with a big, open waiting room. We waited our turn and saw a kind doctor who looked in Emmie's nose and inspected her face. He then mixed up an ointment in a small pot and gave us powder to mix with water for her to drink.

Within a day, the fungus disappeared. I could hardly believe it. Thanks to this doctor and Chinese medicine, my little baby was fixed and fungus-free.

At Sun Moon Lake, after Emmie stubbornly attempted to ride a bike and crashed into a wall, we hired an unusual tandem and rode around the lake together with Emmie sitting on a little seat in front of me. It was a beautiful day and we rode for hours, squealing out horn noises as we overtook couples meandering along, everyone waving and laughing. As we stopped to catch our breath and have a drink of water, Emmie's tooth fell out.

'Mummy, look! It's a Taiwan tooth!' she yelled from the front seat of the bike. 'Will the tooth fairy find me?' Amazingly, she did. The next evening, Emmie spent her tooth-fairy money on a Winnie-the-Pooh helium balloon from the night markets. So very Taiwan.

Too quickly, it was time to leave. We were off to Borneo to explore more of the amazing country that had a hold on our hearts. We spent a night in a windowless hostel, where I didn't sleep a wink in the fear that we wouldn't be able to escape in a fire, and at 5.00 am we trotted off down the road to the bus station. We were so slow and the pack was so heavy, I worried we might miss the bus. I flagged down a taxi and the driver took us to the bus station, dropping us at the wrong entrance, of course. The security guard wouldn't let us in, so we ran around the building to a side entrance and found the airport express ticket counter. The bus was leaving in five minutes and there was no one there!

'She is in the toilet,' a woman at another counter told me.

'Where is it?' I yelled in panic and raced off to the doorway she pointed out, as the people behind the counters laughed at me and Emmie yelled encouragement. The toilets were down three flights of stairs and I raced down them, grabbed the lady who was taking selfies in the bathroom, and we ran back to the counter. She quickly issued our tickets, and we just made it onto the bus.

Emmie curled up with her head in my lap, and I listened to The Sundays as we sped down the motorway. Taiwan was awesome. I was happy my ear had brought us here.

Emmie's Winnie-the-Pooh balloon made it all the way back to the airport with us, but wasn't allowed on the flight. We left it behind, deflated and wrinkled, as we set off for our next adventure.

CHAPTER 7

Always more to learn

Returning to Malaysian Borneo was special for us; it had been part of our journey from the beginning. We'd loved our time here just six months before, and we were keen to explore some more. Coming back to the place that had given us the confidence to tackle our big adventure made our hearts happy.

'And here we are,' we said together as we landed at Kota Kinabalu airport. We emerged into the heat, a welcome change from the coolness of Taiwan.

'Hello, Borneo,' Emmie said. 'I'm so happy to see you.'

We took a taxi to the Shangri-La Tanjung Aru Resort, where we were staying for a few days. It was a thrill to arrive at the resort after staying at so many hostels and guesthouses. I looked like a bit of a dag in my baggy old dress and thongs, but Emmie looked cute so I figured that she balanced us out. I always pack my oldest clothes when we travel, because they get worn out, they don't get washed a lot and they're carried around in the backpack. It's the backpackers' way of doing things that I never moved on from. I probably should have improved that for the resort stays. Oops.

My ear was feeling good and I had bought new earplugs, so I was pretty sure I'd be able to hit the pool and the ocean, albeit carefully. We spent the next two days swimming, drinking coconut milk, collecting frangipanis and shooting down the resort's awesome waterslides. Emmie had so much fun sliding, and double the fun watching me as my extra weight made me go so fast, I was like a torpedo. Look out below! Emmie even spent a bit of time in the Kids' Club while I had a cocktail at the Sunset Bar and relaxed. It was exactly what I needed after more than a month on the road. A little break, a little luxury and a little drink.

Our days at the resort came to an end, and we set off on a week-long trip around Sabah, the land beneath the wind, at the invitation of Sabah Tourism. In return, we were sharing it on our Instagram account. It was the first time we'd worked with a tourism agency, and I was thrilled and nervous. I was slowly starting to understand the opportunities that platforms like Instagram could bring us.

We cruised along in a little minivan with our guide Sylvester, whom Emmie called Victor (she has this weird problem with names), and our driver Adnan. Sylvester is one of the last full-blood descendants of Sabah's Sungai tribe, with an amazing ability to spot and communicate with wildlife, and Adnan was the sweetest, safest driver in town. Driving out of Kota Kinabalu with Emmie's favourite *Pitch Perfect* soundtrack blaring, we quickly hit the open road, passing small villages and jungle, with the majestic Mount Kinabalu always towering in the distance.

Sabah was an incredible adventure for us. It was even more than we expected, with stunning white-sand beaches, clear blue water and some of the best diving in the world. We met tribe members living in longhouses under the guidance of a chief and traditional rules and laws. We spotted endemic wildlife in the jungle: orangutans, proboscis monkeys and pygmy elephants. We paid our respects at memorials to soldiers held in prison camps and sent on the Sandakan Death Marches in World War II by the Japanese, where only six of the 2400 Australian and British troops survived. We ate the most delicious pineapple we'd ever tasted. We learned about headhunters and poison darts and ancient myths and legends. Our eyes were opened to the diversity and history of this rugged Malaysian island.

We sat together in the back of the minivan as we rolled and bumped our way across the state, with Sylvester teaching us about his home. We visited the Mari Mari Cultural Village, where we blew poison darts and learned about ancient tribes, such as the rice wine-making Dusun, the headhunting Merut and the farmers of the Lundayeh and Rungus tribes. It was a window into another world that hadn't completely disappeared. Borneo was clutching its tribal history close and sharing it with us.

Beneath the slopes of Mount Kinabalu, we discovered a rare rafflesia—the biggest flower in the world—and in Kota Belud, we fished and Emmie played with local kids on bamboo rafts while I hung out with their families on the riverbank. Ever generous, they offered me food and drink, and I promised myself to be more open to strangers I met at home. We traced some of the steps of the Sandakan Death March through the Sabah Tea Gardens in Ranau, where we met the grandson of a villager who had helped the escaped Australian prisoners of war, and we visited the memorials to our brave soldiers. Emmie's education was here, in our everyday travels. These experiences were far more valuable than counting in twos, and I knew that she was getting everything she needed from our life on the road.

We travelled to the Tip of Borneo, where the Sulu and South China Seas meet, passing through lines of palms on repeat as far as we could see. When I noticed the symmetry of the plantations, I realised that most of the palms were not natural groves but palm oil plantations. While plantations in Sabah are mostly run by big corporations, families and communities can also make a good living from having their own crop. It's easy to tell who has a plantation, as their houses and villages are usually bigger and fancier. The tragedy is that for these plantations to be built, jungle needs to be cleared. This means wildlife, including majestic creatures such as orangutans, lose their homes and often their lives, especially since a lot of clearing is done by burning to raze the jungle completely. Villages generally don't have a huge amount of land, but big corporations do, and they make a fortune as the world loses wildlife, ancient rainforests and jungle. Sabah has declared the remaining forest and jungle protected to help the orangutans and other wildlife recover and thrive. It has to work; too much has been lost already.

On our way, we stopped to meet Zulah, a 75-year-old Bajau tribe machete, or *parang*, maker. We watched him heat scavenged metal over coals and knock it into shape on an old anvil while he let Emmie blow the bellows for him. We met beekeepers producing organic honey, and farmers growing produce to feed the island. We visited with a family of gong-makers, whose ancestors had learned their craft from Chinese traders and passed it down over the generations, tuning the gongs by ear. We spent time with families in traditional longhouses and learned how they live together. We visited the Sepilok Orangutan Rehabilitation Centre, where young orangutans came down through the trees to eat fresh fruit left at a feeding station—one tried to grab the beads in Emmie's hair—and we watched orphaned babies learn to swing from ropes and play together. We watched sun bears saved from the hideous bile trade snuffle through ground cover for fruit and insects, and visited Gomantong Cave, filled with bat poo and cockroaches, where swiftlet nests are harvested for the bird spit used in their nest-making, valued for its flavour and (supposed) health benefits.

After more than a week of exploring, we arrived at a thatched riverside hut on the Kinabatangan River, the second-longest river in Malaysia. The jungle here is where much of Sabah's wildlife hangs out, and we were desperate to spot pygmy elephants and wild orangutans. Each morning and afternoon, we would climb into a little boat and set off down the mighty Kinabatangan, Emmie and me sitting on the cold metal seats and competing to see who could spot the most. Pygmy elephants foraged on the banks and quickly crossed the river in a long line, almost-hidden crocodiles watched us with lazy eyes, proboscis monkeys crashed through the trees and orangutans sat on branches eating fruit while hornbills majestically flew in pairs across the sky.

One evening, I was the lone guest on a night-time nature walk with a local ranger. In long pants and leech-proof socks and boots, we crept through the bush until a cracking noise broke the silence and stopped the guide in his tracks. He turned to me looking terrified and whispered dramatically, 'Ele-pants are coming. We go back. Now.' Unaware of how serious it was, I had a little giggle.

The herd was on the move and, while they looked small and cute, these elephants could easily trample us. We began a quick trot, now and then stopping commando-style behind trees for the guide to listen for the herd. I thought it was hilarious, only because I totally underestimated how serious an elephant trampling could be. As we emerged back at the huts, Emmie ran along the wooden pathway to meet me, sparkling in the golden glow of the lamps that lined the handrails.

'Mum, what did you see? Did you get a leech on you?'

'No, babe, we had to run from the elephants! They're in the bush just behind us, can you believe it?' I told the story to Emmie, and we laughed about me in my long leech socks running from elephants. Little experiences like these were all part of our journey, sewn into the fabric of our adventure together. We waited quietly to see if the elephants would come closer, but all we saw was a wild boar snuffling in the long grass below the walkway. Still, very exciting!

⌣

Our travels in Borneo reminded me of my backpacking days. The country is still relatively untouched, and many lead a simple life in the villages, living off the land. Emmie and I were starting to get a real taste of a world that was so different from ours at home, and also how welcoming communities and children can be to travellers. At the Taun Gusi Village Homestay in Kota Belud, we spent an afternoon in fits of laughter playing Uno with Sylvester, Adnan and Mr Ismail, the distinguished owner of the home. We were so different in gender, age, race, income, opportunities and religion, and yet laughter and Uno brought us all together. It is one of my fondest memories of our time there.

Always the Uno master, Emmie would reveal her penalty cards with an exaggerated flourish.

'Pick up four, Victor,' she'd announce delightedly to Sylvester.

'His name is Sylvester!' we would scream with laughter as he added a card to pass on the growing penalty.

We left Sylvester and flew back to Mulu for a few nights. I was desperate to see the bat exodus at Gunung Mulu National Park, the one that we'd been rained out on six months earlier. We repeated our climb up the mountain and sat at the mouth of Deer Cave, waiting for the bats to fly. As the sun went down, a trickle turned into a swirling brown ribbon as millions of bats flew from the cave and twirled up high into the sky.

'The bats, the bats,' crooned Emmie. 'The beautiful bats.' It was worth coming back for.

Later, down on the east coast, we snorkelled at Pulau Mabul and swam with Bajau Laut children in the ocean, learning about the lives of this nomadic, ocean-dwelling tribe. The Bajau Laut, or sea gypsies, are from the Sulu Archipelago in the Philippines and live on the sea in canoes and floating homes. Many have now come ashore and live in poverty on the water's edge in stateless communities. Their presence is usually ignored— meaning, they can stay, but have no access to welfare, health services or education.

On Mabul, the kids ran around nude or in ill-fitting clothes, swimming, playing games with coins, plastic bottles and dead fish, and holding their hands out to tourists for food and money. They had many black teeth and were skinny, with long brown legs and swollen little bellies. Older girls wore white paste on their faces made from rice powder to protect their skin from the sun.

The men fished and repaired canoes and holes in the roofs and walls of their one-room stilt houses, built out of scavenged materials. The women waded through waist-deep water collecting sea urchins to trade for food, prepared meals and looked after their children and extended family. We passed on as much as we could from our packs: a bag of apples, colouring books and pencils, a swimming cossie, shorts and a top. Emmie's Barbie sandals went missing overnight, so one little scallywag may have had a new pair of shoes. We didn't mind at all.

It was here in Mabul that I started to feel that it is wrong to take photos of children. I was asking these kids or their parents if I could take their photo, and they were agreeing, but later I realised that they were incapable of knowing what that meant. Why did I want photos of children in poverty anyway? Yes, they were beautiful children living a simple life in nature, but poverty shouldn't be romanticised. These kids and their families had difficult, challenging lives. I found the Bajau Laut fascinating, but taking their photos was wrong and so disrespectful. I realised that their parents would have no idea that the photos may be used on the internet, and I felt like I was exploiting them for potential 'likes' on social media. Even asking the parents' permission wasn't right—Western tourists are in a position of power, and it's not an equal negotiation. I wouldn't walk up to a child at home and take their photo, or ask a mum walking down the street if I could photograph her baby. Why was I doing it here? Why was it okay to take photos of kids in poverty?

It wasn't okay.

I deleted the photos I'd taken, and I haven't taken photos of children since.

We returned to Kota Kinabalu, where it was stinking hot. Emmie and I sweated it out in a hostel with a shared bathroom and no pool. We needed the ocean, so we decided to spend our last day in Borneo on Sapi Island, about twenty minutes from the mainland. We took a boat over and, just as I was getting ready for a relaxing swim, Emmie spotted wires hanging across the water. My heart sank. Of all the islands here, we'd come to the one with a zipline. A skinny wire was strung between Sapi and its neighbour, Gaya Island, 235 metres across the sparkling blue-green water. According to Emmie, it was just waiting for a mama and her child to fly on.

Oh no, here we go again, I thought.

'Mum, you know what this means,' Emmie crowed. 'You're going on the zipline!'

'Noooooooooooo. Oh come on, Emmie, haven't I done enough for you? This is way too much. I'm not going over the water,' I laughed, but I was serious. I didn't want to do it.

Standing on the white sand, under a blue sky in the hot sun, Emmie started the negotiation. 'Mum, it's only $30 each for this zipline with your daughter. We can yell out our happiness! Mum, my fungus is gone and your ear is better and we're together! I can't go on it alone, so you have to come with me.'

'Well, that's not a bad argument . . .' I paused to consider it. *Argh, should I do this?* I realised that I really didn't mind too much. It was over water, so if I fell off or made the zipline collapse, landing in water would be okay. I gave in and we bought our tickets, signed the waiver and hopped into the boat over to Gaya Island. We followed a sandy path up to a small hut, where we stopped to get fitted into our gear.

'You two will go together, mama and baby,' the blokes running it told us as I hooked my dress into my cossie bottoms and we stepped into our harnesses. 'Now, up the path and we get you ready to fly.'

We walked along a dirt track and then climbed up to a small platform high above the stunning channel of turquoise water between the islands. We reached the top and, all of a sudden, we were being hooked up to the wire. I had no time to process what was going on and prepare myself. We were attached and my bum was resting on something, but I felt unstable and started freaking out. The men were trying to get me to sit down properly, but I just couldn't lift my feet off the ground.

'Are you sure I won't break it?' I asked frantically, heart thumping.

'It's good, it's good. Just lift your feet,' they told me. But I couldn't. I was sure I was going to fall off. I'd had a terrifying parasailing experience with Emmie where my bum was hanging over the back of the seat and I swore I was going to slide off, and this felt exactly like that! Yes, it was funny, but I felt strongly that my life was at risk. My dignity had already slipped away.

'I can't! I don't feel safe. I have to get off.' The boys were frustrated, and the person behind me groaned in annoyance, but I jumped off and someone else was hooked up and sailed off over the water.

'Oh, come on, Mum! This is embarrassing,' Emmie whispered as I tried to shake it off. 'This is our happy zipline! We are happy, and we are going to have fun. You can do it.'

Oh jeez. I climbed back on, remembering the zipline magic from Bohol.

I can do this, I told myself. *I am good enough, I am strong, I am happy. Plus, if I fall off, there is water below to break my fall.*

The men released us, and we sailed through the air from Gaya Island over to Sapi, above stunning blue-green water, free as birds and happy as clams.

'You're doing it, Mum,' yelled Emmie. 'We are happy! We are happy!'

Within seconds we reached Sapi Island and landed on a little platform above the trees.

'Mum, you did it!' Emmie yelled as she gave me a hug. 'Let's do it again!'

Back at the beach, we swam and snorkelled in the clear blue water until the last boat was ready to take the stragglers back to the big island. It was a fabulous last day in Borneo.

⌣

Jacqui was living in an apartment in River Valley in Singapore, and we headed there for a big catch-up. Emmie and I were two-and-a-half months into our trip, and it was so good to spend time with Jacqui. I was looking forward to a little splash of the familiar and a big splash of bubbles from her champagne fridge.

'Welcome, Muriel,' she greeted me as we arrived, using the nickname we'd been given on our backpacking trip after a particularly big night in Singapore with some awesome Kiwi backpackers.

'Well, hello Muriel, so good to see you!' I replied with a big hug.

'Moo Moo,' Emmie yelled as she grabbed her godmother and me for a big group cuddle.

Jacqui's partner Jav was working in London for a few weeks, so it was just the girls. The champagne was poured and we were straight into it, catching up on our lives and reminiscing about all the fun we'd had over the past 30 years, while Emmie got stuck into doing what she'd missed the most: watching TV. Jacqui is so much fun, her ability to drink champagne is legendary and her energy never stops. I am the opposite, the messy one, the naughty one, the Nicole to her Paris, the Michele to her Romy. It was great to see her.

I get asked all the time if I'm lonely while we travel because it's just me and Emmie all day, every day. Honestly, I couldn't have been further from being lonely. Emmie and I were constantly having fun, exploring, learning and doing something new. We met so many inspiring, like-minded people on the road who didn't care if I was a solo mum, or if I had two heads. We found our people—or we didn't find anyone, and it was just the two of us, bumbling along, enjoying life and discovering the world as we went. No stress, no deadlines, just living and loving every minute. Plus, social media made it easy to stay in touch with family and new and old friends while we explored. I had so much support from our friends who lived inside my phone, and I loved it.

For me, being on the road was less lonely than being at home. I used to dread weekends when we didn't have plans or invitations, when Facebook was full of show-reels of two-parent families having so much fun, enjoying parties and weekends away together. I would have loved to be included, but it felt like we were forgotten, or there wasn't room for a solo mum at the table. At home, I didn't have a feeling of belonging, of being loved and included, but when we were travelling I did because we set our direction, we were in control and no one was leaving us out. Plus, everyone was different on the road, and there was that same beautiful travellers' acceptance that I'd felt when backpacking almost twenty years earlier.

The next day was Anzac Day, one of the most important dates on the Australian and New Zealand calendars. It's so important to me that Emmie is aware of the women and men who sacrificed their lives so that we could have freedom and independence, and she has been to the Dawn Service every year since she was born. Jacqui drove us all out to the service at Changi Museum, and we talked to Emmie about our visit to Gallipoli almost twenty years earlier. As usual, it was a very emotional morning.

After a few more nights of champagne, hawker markets and museum visits, it was time to leave Jacqui and Singapore, and get back on the road. I started packing up our bags, which had exploded all over Jacqui's spare room. As usual, it was part jigsaw— fitting everything into its place—and part force, just shoving when stuff wouldn't fit. When we were flying, my daypack held our passports, my camera and computer, a book and other bits and bobs like baby wipes. When we were exploring, it was full of water, sunscreen, a camera, hats and bandaids. Emmie's daypack had all manner of crap she had managed to stuff in there when I wasn't looking. It was a source of tension for us, given that she barely used any of the junk she just *had* to have, and I had to carry it most of the time. I felt some leniency, since it was all she had of her own for a year, but I drew the line when she started adding rocks.

'Mum, I need it all. Trust me,' she would say, staring at me intently, willing me to let her have her way.

'Nope, sorry.' I'd tip out the rocks, shells (Shells! She knew very well we don't take shells from their home!), torn-up pieces of paper and general rubbish.

I never found everything, though. There would always be a hidden pebble or some other piece of detritus in her bag. Once, I found an old rotting pippy in a side pocket, a fishy stench taking over the air as I pulled it out. It was lucky we weren't heading back into Australia, or Border Patrol would have been onto us.

I stuffed the backpack full once again and hoisted it onto my back while Emmie filled her bag with knick-knacks and rubbish, and off we went. I'd found $40 flights into Ipoh on Skyscanner, about halfway between Malaysia's capital, Kuala Lumpur, and Penang. I researched a little and found that there were cave temples in the limestone mountains, a famous bean sprout chicken specialty at the hawker markets, and a randomly big Sunway theme park beneath the hills. It was enough for us, and the perfect trade-off with Emmie—a day of cave temples would equal a day at the theme park.

Ipoh was an hour's flight from Singapore on the Malaysian airline Firefly. At the check-in counter, we had the usual budget-flight trauma of carrying overweight bags. The packing and repacking panic at check-in was not unusual for us. Most of the time, we would need to spread the weight out onto our bodies or into our daypacks. Sometimes the staff would get us to reduce the weight of the pack, weigh it in and then let us put the extra kilos back in. Not this time, though. We had three kilos to reduce, so I opened the pack and it exploded around us, a sea of packing cubes, random clothing, a hairbrush, toiletries, our snorkels and those hideous blue schoolwork folders. I moved things around and shoved a packing cube into my handbag, praying I'd be able to get the pack shut again. I was panicked and holding up the queue, and in the middle of my sweaty chaos, I heard Emmie yelling, 'Mum, watch this' and 'Watch me, Mum' as she ran across the floor twenty metres away, throwing her Elf on the Shelf in the air and dodging people as they walked along with their suitcases. *Oh, God help me.*

While we waited to board our flight, I booked the cheapie Ritz Garden Hotel in Ipoh. As we walked in a few hours later, our host Dave rushed over to greet us.

'Hello, hello, thank you. We are so happy you are here.' Dave was so sweet and proudly showed us around this lovely and perplexing budget hotel, with its spiral staircase, in-house movie theatre and huge swimming pool surrounded by rock gardens and waterfalls.

'If you want to watch a movie, if you want anything, just call me on the telephone.' He grabbed us some towels and we changed into our cossies and spent the morning playing Marco Polo and chasings in the pool before heading out to the cave temples in a little taxi with a sweet old driver.

'Where do you come from?' he asked us.

'We're from Australia,' Emmie answered proudly.

'Ah, I have family in Australia. My nephew studies in Melbourne. Very good place.'

'Oh, what is he studying? Does he love it? Have you visited?'

Most Malaysians seem to have family in Australia, or have studied there, or have relatives at university. They just love talking about it and connecting, and we did, too. We chatted all the way to the cave temples, and our driver told us all about them. Over thousands of years, water had flowed through the limestone mountains that surround Ipoh, creating passageways and huge caverns with soaring ceilings and hidden rooms carved out of the rock. The Chinese who came to Ipoh made Buddhist and Taoist temples in these caves, and it makes sense— the coolness is calming, and the peacefulness inside the limestone feels deeply spiritual.

I was keen to see the cave temples and get a hit of Buddhism goodness. Kek Long Tong, the Temple of Ultimate Bliss, was our first stop. We climbed the stairs past statues of Buddha, miniature scenes carved out of stone and ornate sculptures of dragons to a huge jagged opening, the entrance to the cave. We had this mystical limestone cavern all to ourselves. A breeze blew through the entrance to another huge hole at the back of the cave, leading out to beautiful gardens and a view over the valley below. Golden statues of Buddha and Taoist deities lined the walls, and huge stalactites hung down from the ceiling. Both Emmie and I felt soothed by a sense of peace and the coolness of the caves.

Next, at the colourful Nam Thean Tong temple, the Cave of the Southern Sky, Emmie discovered some old stairs carved into the rock, leading upwards. 'Mum, come here,' she whispered to me, and we scrambled up a narrow passageway into ancient monks' quarters and places of worship, and gazed out over the valley below.

We wandered through gardens full of painted statues of the Chinese zodiac under colourful flowering trees and golden archways, and delighted in finding life-size sculptures of Monkey King and his disciples. We stood under the wishing tree and, while Emmie annoyingly wished for Disneyland, I wished for a child who would be helpful and work with me to get her schoolwork done. I felt blessed we'd had these caves and temples to ourselves, and felt recharged and at peace again.

After two days of temples plus chicken and bean sprouts at the local hawker markets and satay sticks from roadside stalls, we visited Sunway's Lost World of Tambun, as promised. Again, there was hardly anyone around. We rode amusements from the 1980s and spent hours on the waterslides.

The next day, we set off for Penang Island, and the food and famous street art of George Town, taking the long-distance bus to the Butterworth ferry terminal for the trip over to the island. I had no idea how we would get across, but an older Aussie bloke across the aisle gave me all the details (which, of course, turned out to be totally wrong).

'G'day, love,' he said, ready for a chat. 'I'm Greg, and this is my girlfriend Simone.' He flicked his thumb towards the woman staring out of the window next to him. Dropping his voice and raising his eyebrows, he announced, 'She's a ladyboy.'

Omg, I thought. *What an idiot.*

'Hi there, nice to meet you. I'm Evie and this is Emmie. Hi Simone!'

I'm not sure Greg got the reaction he expected, but after a short pause, he continued. 'I know a lot of men who come here for them. I left my wife for one. They're the perfect species, the brains of a man and the body of a woman. I can talk about football and get a … ' He paused and whispered, 'root.'

'Right, that's so awesome for you,' I replied, far from impressed. I tried to turn away, but Greg kept talking and began telling me about his nephew's search for a girlfriend.

'It's not easy for him to find a good woman. He has to shop around, you know?' he said. 'I mean, you wouldn't go into a car yard and buy the first one you saw, would you? You need to take it for a test-drive. It's just like women, you have to test them out first.'

'Sorry, Greg, but that's enough for me,' I said, cutting him off. 'Women aren't cars, we're not objects. I'm sure Simone would agree. Thanks for the chat, but I'm tired and I'm going to have a snooze for the rest of the trip.' He seemed confused, but the conversation was over.

It is tough to be bringing up a daughter in a world where women are so often seen as commodities, as less-than, and are still treated that way. I was angry and frustrated with Greg. We were feeling so empowered, but Greg's prejudice brought me back to reality, reminding me of all the challenges women still face. It made me more determined than ever to bring Emmie up as a strong and independent young woman.

After four hours on the bus, we arrived at the ferry terminal. As Greg led Simone in the wrong direction up the side of the freeway, Emmie and I followed the other passengers to the ferry terminal and crossed the Penang Strait to George Town. We trudged down the jetty with our backpacks and jumped in a cab to the hostel I'd booked. Taxis were so cheap in Malaysia, and I'd shaken off the backpacker mentality of avoiding paying for transport. Back in the day, Jacqui and I would walk for miles with our overloaded packs to save a dollar. There was no way I was going to do that now, especially in the desperate heat of Penang.

We had the run of the house at the hostel, with no one else in the shared bathrooms, kitchen or loungeroom. It was awesome, but I regretted not splurging and getting somewhere with a pool. It was so hot. Even so, we felt safe and happy in Penang, like we belonged. Emmie and I discovered a few places that felt like this in our travels. We call them our spirit towns, and Penang was one of them.

We roamed Penang's streets, sweating and loving the diversity of George Town—buying sweets in Little India, scoffing our favourite Hainanese chicken rice sitting on plastic chairs and tables in tiny crowded shops full of local families, eating delicious chilli pork and plates of broccoli and beans at the Tek Sen restaurant and chatting to the family who had started it in 1965 as a little rice shop. We wandered the night markets and visited as many temples as we could. I fell in love with the coloured doorways and walls, and the detail of the heavy gates pulled across the fronts of houses and businesses each evening.

'Mum, is today the day?' Emmie asked a few days after we arrived.

'Today is the day, Emmie,' I answered. 'Have you got your pedalling legs on?'

'I sure have. Let's go!'

We were off to ride one of the now-banned big yellow quadricycles around the streets on the beloved George Town street art route. These bikes were like big metal chariots, using pedal power and steering wheels to carry tourists all over town to the beautiful, quirky paintings on the sides of buildings. We hired our bike and slowly pedalled off. We both had a wheel and it was tandem decision-making time.

'Oh my God, pedal, Emmie! Reverse! Stop pedalling. Go forward! Oh no.'

'Turn the wheel, Mum! Sorry, sorry people. Here we come!' Emmie honked the horn and we laughed and apologised as we made our way around the streets. The locals in cars were so patient with everyone—there were literally hundreds of us trying to work our big yellow bikes, laughing and stopping at the street art, eating flavoured shaved ice and dodging all the other quadricycles.

It was hot and sticky as we walked down the street to the hostel that afternoon. Emmie had wanted to light incense and say a little prayer, so we had visited the Taoist Goddess of Mercy temple on the way, adding a few kilometres to our tally for the day.

I'm usually always hot, but this was intense, and my growing thighs squished and stuck together with every step.

'Mum, I'm boiling,' Emmie moaned. 'Can we please get an ice-cream?' When she felt the heat, I knew it was hot, so we stopped at the little shop at the end of our street to grab a treat.

'*Salamat tengah hari, apa kabar?*' we greeted the man at the counter who had come to know us from our afternoon lolly runs. We got the usual, a Cornetto for Emmie and packet of M&Ms for me, and wandered home. As we walked through the guesthouse door, I put the packet in my mouth to rip it open and felt my front tooth twist and shift.

What was that? 'Oh my God! Emmie, look at my tooth, look at my tooth—is it okay?' I bared my teeth at her, freaking out that my tooth was falling out and too scared to touch it.

'Hmm, let me see, Patient Mummy.' As she inspected it, I tapped it with my tongue and felt it move. It was twisted and felt like it was about to fall out.

'Mum, you've broken your tooth trying to rip open your chocolate. What will you do? I can't have a mum with one tooth!'

The tooth was a fake that had replaced my real one after I had faceplanted trying to ride my scooter down at our caravan a few months before our trip. I'd landed on my head and banged my tooth, which sadly went grey and had to go. Only a small part of my real tooth was left, poking out of my gum like a thin discoloured fang. I'd always felt my replacement tooth was dodgy, but it had cost a fortune from a supposedly reputable dentist at home—seems I'd been right, though, since it was now hanging out of my mouth.

Emmie gazed at me with glowing eyes, delighted at the drama. 'Mum, what if you have to walk around with one tooth for the rest of our trip? How will you charm people? How will you eat?'

I called the hostel owner, who put me in touch with a dentist a few kilometres away, and off we trekked down a dusty old street to a small glass shopfront right on the footpath. Inside was a tiny waiting room full of people, a huge fish tank and a small desk with a lovely receptionist who sent us upstairs for my appointment.

Emmie freaked out when I lay in the dentist's chair. I was also freaking out about potentially having only one front tooth, especially when the dentist tried to remove the broken falsie and couldn't get the last piece off. He called the big boss, who inserted a metal instrument into my mouth and, with a flick of his wrist, catapulted the remnants of the fake tooth across the room. I was left with the tiny prong of my original tooth sticking out.

'Let me see, Mum, let me see!' yelled Emmie, desperate to look at me with only one front tooth. She made me smile to show her, and I'm thankful she didn't have my phone or I'm sure she would have taken a photo and beamed it to the world.

'Oh, Mummy.' She started crying. 'I don't like it! Please get another tooth on there!'

'That's what I'm trying to do, Emmie!' I gave her a big hug from the dentist chair and handed her my phone, which she played on for the rest of the appointment.

The dentists made a mould of my tooth, shoved a temporary fake one in and told me to come back in two weeks. Oh well, no problem. We would have to re-route, but we had all the time in the world, thank goodness.

'Righto, Emmie, new tooth attached. Let's get to the beach!'

We made our way over to Koh Lipe in Thailand, taking $10 flights into Langkawi and exploring there for a week before jumping onto a ferry. It didn't really make sense since we couldn't continue on further into Thailand now, but I'd heard so much about this little island and desperately wanted to go. Staying in a hut right on the beach was the perfect way to spend time on Koh Lipe, although it was stinking hot so we immediately upgraded to an air-conditioned one. We snorkelled over coloured corals and picnicked on deserted white sandy islands, we swam and watched the sun set into the ocean over the colourful long-tail boats tied up on the beach. Emmie searched for hermit crabs and collected shells and rocks for sand-cake decorating, and we built castles and coral towers. It was so calm that we even had a schoolwork breakthrough as we sat on the beach under a bamboo shade, reading and relaxing.

Thai food was delicious. I loved the curries and couldn't get enough. After devouring a spicy vegetable dish one night, I saw Emmie looking at me with a huge smile on her face and trouble in her eyes. I smiled back, and she burst out laughing.

'Mum, what's your favourite colour?' she asked me.

'It's blue, honey. You know that, the same as yours.'

'No, Mummy, my new favourite colour is yellow. Do you want to know why?'

'Why?'

'Because it's the same colour as your new tooth!' She burst out laughing.

What? *Oh no.* The bloody yellow turmeric curry had absorbed into the fake tooth. I looked at it in my phone and swore. My tooth was yellow. All the brushing in the world couldn't fix that. *Well, at least I have a tooth,* I tried to look on the bright side.

At this point, I had completed my regression into a dodgy backpacker. I had a yellow tooth, I had lost my deodorant paste and was rubbing lime under my arms, I was sweating constantly in daggy old clothes, my undies had holes in them, my nail polish was chipped and I was pretty hairy. But I'd found my sweet spot. After almost four months of travelling, it was here at Koh Lipe that my mind and my body relaxed. I stopped clenching my teeth and holding my breath. I wasn't standing so rigidly, my mind had slowed right down and I just felt softer, less busy. It had taken a while, but I'd shaken off the anxiety and pace of home. It felt good.

After a week of bliss, it was time to move on. We packed up our bags and grabbed a tuk tuk to the other side of the island. Immigration was a small hut on the beach, and we exited Thailand and jumped on a boat back to Malaysia. From Langkawi, we took another super cheap flight to Kuala Lumpur to apply for our China visas. We were crisscrossing Malaysia again, but it couldn't be helped; the tooth meant that instead of an overland meander through Thailand, we were staying put.

I lost sight of Emmie at Langkawi airport as we waited for the plane, but there weren't many places she could go, so I wasn't too worried. When I spotted her sitting on the ground, part of a circle of Muslim women dressed in their hijabs, I smiled and wandered over to say hello. She had joined their card game and they were all laughing, patting her hair and teaching her how to play. Moments like these made me happy.

With our China visa application submitted in Kuala Lumpur, we returned to Penang. Hooray! Today I was getting a new white tooth. I lay in the dentist's chair, and he popped it in.

'Take a look,' he said proudly, giving me a mirror.

The tooth was pink.

'Ha ha, Mum, your tooth is pink,' Emmie laughed. 'Pink like those pink dolphins. Let me throw you a fish.'

'This is not really what I expected,' I told the dentist in a huge panic. 'The tooth is pink! We need another one.'

'Okay, okay.' He called the senior dentist in, and there was a flurry of Bahasa and phone calls.

Oh God, please let them give me a new tooth, I prayed. They could easily say no, and I'd have to live with a pink tooth, which I wasn't convinced was a step up from a yellow one.

The dentist finished his phone call and came over with his iPhone—another medical iPhone!—and took a photo of my teeth for more 'colour-matching'. He put the turmeric tooth back on my fang, and we were done for the day.

'Come back tomorrow for your new tooth,' he said with a smile.

What to do when you're waiting for a tooth? Emmie had been wanting to go up to the top of Penang Hill on the funicular, a train that climbs steeply up the side of the mountain with scary views straight down. I'd read that there were beautiful views from the top and nice walks through the jungle and gardens, so off we set. We caught an Uber to the bottom of the hill and jumped on the funicular, snagging the coveted front seat. Up we went, inching up between the rock and jungle, dragged almost vertically up the mountainside, sliding forward in our seats and hanging, gazing down.

'Yeah, I love this!' screamed Emmie. 'Are you scared, Mummy?'

At the top, we alighted to a deserted information centre, and the few people in the car with us quickly disappeared. We didn't know where to go, so we played Paper, Scissors, Rock to choose a direction and set off along the path to the right, emerging into jungle. After a few steps, we came face to face with a bunch of manky, menacing macaques. They were all shapes and sizes, in the trees and on the handrails. Small ones were playing, and the huge patriarch was standing aggressively in the centre, his big, sharp teeth bared at us.

'Mum, what do we do?' Emmie whispered, panicking and grabbing my hand.

I didn't know. I hate those hideous creatures. They are erratic, desperate opportunists, the rats of the monkey world. You never know what they are going to do. One second they can be sitting nonchalantly and the next, they're attacking.

'Don't look them in the eyes, Emmie, and keep walking!' was the only advice I had. As we shuffled forward in an attempt to pass them, the pack of feral grey beasts ran towards us. We quickly retreated.

'It's okay, Emmie, we can ask someone to help us. The staff will know what to do and if it's safe,' I told her, and we went back to the funicular station where we found the driver who had just brought the next train in.

'Excuse me?' asked Emmie. 'Can you please help us get past the macaques? We hate them, and we're scared.'

'Yes, of course,' he said, with a heroic spring in his step. 'Just follow me.'

Our rescuer was very confident, swinging his little blue briefcase as he approached the monkey gang with us creeping behind him.

Our fearless leader took a few steps closer and then suddenly, the monkeys attacked! He fended them off with his briefcase before turning and sprinting past us, screaming as they chased him. Emmie and I stared at each other in shock.

'Oh my God, Emmie. *RUN!*' I screamed and turned back to the funicular. After a few steps, to my horror, I realised my little buddy was not beside me. I'd left her. *Oh the shame!* I had left my baby behind to be attacked by wild macaques. What was I thinking? I guess I wasn't thinking. I turned to see her stuck to the spot in fear as the smaller monkeys pawed her legs and the big male paced in front of her.

'Leave her alone!' I yelled as I ran back, swinging my camera at them and grabbing Emmie's hand. We made it to the station and safety, but the driver was nowhere to be found. I assumed he was hiding from us or still running.

'Okay, that's it. No more jungle or gardens or walking for us. We are done!' I told Emmie.

'Muuummm, you left me,' she said, looking at me with indignation. 'How could you leave your one and only daughter!' She had a few tiny marks on her shins but no broken skin, thank goodness.

'I'm so sorry, baby, I thought you were right behind me,' I told her. Well, that kind of wasn't true. In that moment, I didn't even think, it was every man for himself. Not my proudest mum moment.

I had to fix this immediately. 'Did you know that there's a famous high-tea cafe up here on the hill, Emmie? Let's go have some special sandwiches and cakes, okay?'

'Are there any monkeys?'

'No monkeys! I promise.'

And that's how Emmie got to have a posh (and expensive) high tea on Penang Hill, and we broke the budget yet again.

The next day, we returned to get my perfectly colour-matched tooth affixed to my fang. I was so happy, especially with the cost, which was a quarter of what it would have been in Australia. It fit better, it looked better, and I now had two permanent top front teeth and could smile as much as I wanted. Success!

CHAPTER 8

The Dragon Team

I first took Emmie to Disneyland when she had just turned two years old. It was a total whim—and the beginning of a love affair that will never end. Disneyland hadn't been on my radar before having Emmie; I'd only wanted to backpack and explore, and was too cynical to believe in the kind of happiness you can find there. I think I found my first big theme park adventure more intimidating than any other kind of travel, but we quickly got the hang of it.

I had booked us into the fancypants Grand Californian Hotel, right next to the park, thinking that we would only visit Disneyland once in our lives, and so we would do this trip well. As we arrived, a pianist was playing Disney theme songs and a cast member smiled at us and said, 'Welcome home', and I just felt this kind of goosebumpy, teary happiness, like I could forget all my worries.

At Disneyland, it was just Emmie and me, and we felt safe and loved. It was—and still is—a very special place for us. Being at Disneyland with Emmie when everything was really tough gave me so much joy. Every morning, I'd get Emmie up early and push her pram down to the gates, ready for a big day ahead. I was so into it that we would always be right at the front of the queue and often the first to enter. We'd zoom around all morning on the rides, meeting Minnie, Mickey and princesses, and then we would go back to the resort and Emmie would have a nap before we hit the park again in the afternoon. Sometimes, I would sit in the beautiful lobby with Emmie asleep on me, just feeling the magic and happiness, stroking her hair, listening to the pianist and often shedding a little tear. We loved our first visit so much, we've gone back every year.

Just before we left on our big trip, I came out of my Disneyland closet to my colleagues. They thought my addiction was hilarious but sharing it paid off, because one day my teammate Naomi came to me with big news.

'Evie, you will not believe this,' she'd said excitedly. 'I've just discovered that Wayne from Accounts is a founding member of the Australian Disneyland Fan Club. I'm setting up a meeting for you!'

A Disneyland fan club? For adults?! I had no idea this was a thing, but sign me up! Naomi introduced us, and Wayne and I were immediately lifelong Disney pals. Wayne briefed me on secret Disney insider tips, and when I stopped by his desk to tell him we were going away for a year on our big trip, he asked if we would be visiting China.

'We sure will be,' I told him. 'Emmie is obsessed with the Great Wall of China after watching *Mulan*, so we are going to be there sometime in the middle of the year.'

'Have you heard about the new Shanghai Disneyland?' he asked me with raised eyebrows and a cheeky grin.

'No.' I was intrigued. 'What have you got to tell me?'

'Meet me in the lunchroom at midday, and I'll give you all the details.'

'Okay, Wayne.' I loved it: a secret meeting! Wayne told me all about the new Shanghai Disneyland—it was fifteen years in the making and finally almost finished. The grand opening was scheduled for June 2016, and the fan club was going. All I had to do was join, and we could go with them.

'Emmie is going to lose her mind over this,' I laughed. It was meant to be.

So we joined our very first fan club and had one date on our trip when we needed to be somewhere: 16 June 2016, the grand opening of Disneyland Shanghai, in China.

And now it was happening—on our way to China from Kuala Lumpur, we stopped at Hong Kong to visit Rajani, her husband and her son John, the friends we'd made on our first stop in the Philippines. It was great to catch up, and we spent the day together on a Chinese junk in Victoria Harbour.

The fan club was in town, too, and we joined them at Hong Kong Disneyland for the day. We were so keen to meet the club! They were exactly as I'd expected—an adorable bunch of Disney-loving men and women aged around 40–60, wearing bumbags, comfortable walking shoes, video cameras and as much Disney memorabilia as possible. At breakfast, we ate cute Piglet-shaped dumplings, met Minnie and Mickey Mouse and then we all went into the park. The fan club had arranged a few special activities while we were inside, all to be enjoyed while wearing our matching Australian Disneyland Fan Club t-shirts. One was walking in the Disneyland parade in front of the huge crowd.

'Um, I'm not sure about that,' I said to the fabulous president Barry and his wife, Narelle.

'Oh Evie, it's such an honour! You have to do it,' they told me. 'You get to walk down Main Street before the parade starts, and everyone watches you and high-fives you.'

Oooh, I didn't want to! *Maybe I could send Emmie off with them and watch from the sidelines?* I thought.

Luckily for us, the Disneyland staff must have been worried about the fan club all making it to the end of the parade route in one piece, and a big red double-decker bus was wheeled out for us. We were given huge Mickey hands to wave, and we all climbed aboard and sailed down the parade route and onto Main Street.

'Mum, look at me,' Emmie yelled, and she held down the fingers in the giant hand so only the 'naughty finger' was up as she jabbed it at people. I just laughed. It was pure Emmie.

A few days later, we arrived in Shanghai and checked into the Toy Story Hotel, welcomed by lines of staff, waving and clapping as we walked in.

'Are we really the first ones at Disneyland Shanghai, Mum?' asked Emmie as we settled into our room.

'We sure are, Emmie! The very first to stay in this room and the first to get into the park. It's incredible.' Everything was going well, which was a huge relief after the media had reported thousands of people swarming the gates, desperate to get in.

The next day, we met up with the Disney gang again, ready for the most exciting day on the Disneyland calendar this decade.

This was it! The opening of Disneyland Shanghai. And off we waddled, wearing our long pants and comfortable shoes, bumbags and Mickey Mouse hats, all in our matching t-shirts. The Australian Disneyland Fan Club was in the house! We strolled through the gates and down Main Street, waving to the hundreds of Disney cast members lining the footpaths, all smiling and saying welcome as we walked past. I had tears of happiness, and Emmie clutched my hand and looked around in awe, waving and yelling 'ni hao' to all the staff.

'Mum, come on! I want to ride on TRON first, and we always start from the back of the park, so let's go!'

Emmie and I spent more than twelve hours running around the park, going on as many rides as we could before the day was over. We hung out with Narelle and Barry, and helped them retrace their steps to find their lost bumbag. We sailed on the Pirates of the Caribbean, screamed on the Seven Dwarfs Mine Train and went Soaring Over the Horizon. There was just so much to see. The next day, we joined a VIP tour with a bunch of people from our fan club and the German Disneyland Fan Club and went straight to the front of the queues, achieving our goal of going on every ride in the park. The fireworks each evening were the most spectacular I'd ever seen, and the people were so kind and friendly, there wasn't any of the overcrowding or pushing we'd been worried about. And although I found it a little amusing, it really was special to share these never-to-be-repeated moments with so many Disney fans from around the world.

As our time in Disneyland came to an end, I once again shoved all our gear in our pack and we set off on the bus and train into Shanghai. Rain was drizzling as we looked for our hostel, a little lost but sure we would find it. I was lugging the pack and the daypacks around as usual and for some reason was wearing my thongs (a very bad footwear choice) when, all of a sudden, my legs were in the air.

'Ooooufff!' I hit the ground.

'Ahhh,' screamed Emmie, laughing as I lay there on the crossing in the middle of a busy Shanghai road, stuck on my back with the pack underneath me, and a very sore big toe. 'You're like a turtle on its shell, Mum. Can you get up? Get up, Mum, get up,' and she pulled my arm, bent over with laughter as I literally couldn't move. I couldn't roll, I couldn't rise; I just couldn't get up.

Suddenly, two elderly Chinese ladies dressed in matching floral tops and pants appeared. Their faces showed that they meant business. Each grabbed an arm and pulled me up, laughing and gesturing how difficult it was to get me off the ground. They pointed to my thongs and shook their heads.

'Oh, I know, I know, silly me!' I said. 'Thank you so much, *xie xie*.' I thanked them as they walked away laughing. And so we continued our China adventure.

China proved to me that the narrow slivers of information I gained about countries and travel from the media, news and internet were so often entirely different to reality. If I'd formed an opinion about China based on that, I'd probably have assumed it was completely industrial, dirty, overcrowded, impolite and unfriendly.

And that is just not true. China is home to breathtakingly beautiful, well-cared-for nature, organised tourist trails, a super easy transport network, delicious food, safe travel and caring, kind people who went out of their way to look after us. Stall owners chased after us to give Emmie fruit, people paid for our taxis, drove us in their cars, offered to show us around their towns and were very kind. China remains Emmie's favourite country. She loves the diversity of experiences we had there—every day in China was an adventure—and, of course, the *xiao long bao*. We adored taking the train, finding our seats or beds and settling into the rhythm of the carriages as we flew past cities, the countryside and huge stations that seemed to jump out of nowhere.

From Shanghai, we took the train to Hangzhou, a beautiful town on West Lake surrounded by immaculate gardens and ancient temples. As we waited in the taxi queue, one of the passengers asked me where we were going and then insisted we join her in her taxi. She took us to the hostel and refused the money we offered, simply wishing us a happy trip.

It poured with rain for three days, so we bummed around the hostel, playing pool with Chinese tourists while we listened to Jack Johnston on the CD player over and over again. The rain stopped for a little bit, so Emmie and I went outside for a walk around the lake. We were crossing a bridge when we heard a duck quacking and looked up to see a man dragging it from the water, twisting its neck and shoving it into a garbage bag.

Oh my God! What is happening? I thought. Then I realised—he was a duck thief! I yelled at him, and he turned for a second, then walked faster as he continued to shove the duck into his bag. No one else cared. I suppose when you're hungry, duck is pretty tempting. I felt like a hypocrite because I was looking forward to my Peking Duck in Beijing, but it was so random and upsetting. Although, maybe it wasn't random. There didn't seem to be any other ducks around …

The next day, we set off to Chengdu on a fourteen-hour train ride. The crew in Carriage 13 were all pretty good friends by the end of it, a camaraderie forged from being so close for so long in those second-class seats. The seats were actually comfortable, the toilet was a squatter—and we love squatters—and the train was tidy, clean and fast. Emmie made a friend on the train, and they shared snacks and practised folding origami. By the end of the trip, Emmie had the whole carriage taking group selfies.

Stiff and tired, we arrived at the Hello Chengdu International Youth Hostel, another fabulous, cheap place to stay. Hostels are so great these days compared to when I was backpacking in the 1990s! There was a restaurant that made Western meals plus awesomely spicy Sichuan dishes, gorgeous little gardens with ponds, tiny bonsai and a fluffy bunny Emmie adored and was rationed time with lest she kill it with cuddles. They had movie nights, table tennis and lots of spots for people to sit around and chat and meet other travellers. Emmie learned magic tricks from young Israeli backpackers and made paper planes with Japanese students.

We visited the Chengdu Research Base of Giant Panda Breeding, where we bumped into a backpacker we'd met in Malaysia a few months before. I love that part of backpacking, the bumping into people you've met in other countries. Twin baby pandas had just been born, and we queued over and over again to shuffle past and look at them being fed and cared for by a team of vets. We roamed around the city, eating spicy meals and exploring the streets, the food stalls and pet shops with turtles in watery tanks.

'Look, Mum, there's you,' said Emmie, pointing at the turtles. 'Remember when you fell over in the street?'

We decided to take a two-day trip from the hostel to the forest, clear lakes and waterfalls at Jiuzhaigou National Park. We set off from the hostel with three other backpackers—Daniel from Israel, Natta from Russia and Gosia from Poland—all strangers on a little adventure together. Like train travel, bus tours in China are in a league of their own, for both efficiency and amusement. We left the hostel in a taxi at around 4.00 am and were dropped at a pick-up point on the side of the road. We bought pork buns and scallion cakes from little stalls and hoped our bus would appear before Emmie fell asleep on the footpath. After another twenty minutes it arrived in a gaggle of tourist buses, with our guide bursting from the door in a cloud of energy to hustle us on for our eight-hour ride to Jiuzhaigou.

We grabbed our seats up the back, the only English speakers in a busload of Chinese tourists, as our guide took the microphone and spent the next three hours screaming into it. I'm sure he had incredibly worthwhile information, but it was 4.30 am, and wow, that decibel level was *high*. We reckoned two of the eight hours of travel was for sales, as we stopped at tourist shops along the way. We were encouraged to buy health tonics, magic jade stones and potions to cure diseases and ease sore muscles. After Emmie's fungus experience, I was tempted, but I saved my pennies. Sometimes, the touts jumped on board and tried to sell to us as we drove through their town. I didn't buy anything, even though I felt sorry for them and admired their tenacity; it couldn't have been an easy job.

The loudness of the microphone was full-on, and we were getting tired of bus-sitting and losing our hearing, so we decided to take the noise levels into our own hands at a tourist stop.

'Emmie, I dare you to unplug the microphone,' I whispered, laughing as we walked down the aisle.

'No, Mum! I might get caught. You do it!' she said with a naughty glint in her eyes.

'No, you do it, Emmie. It's better if a child does it. You won't get in as much trouble as I will if I get caught,' I countered.

'You do it, Mum, I'm just a kid.'

'Okay, okay. I'm doing it. Cover me.' While the guide was off the bus and the driver was stretching his legs, I pulled the microphone cord out and plugged it into a different socket. Emmie and I raced down the back of the bus in fits of laughter, and sat, waiting.

Finally, everyone boarded and the bus started moving.

'Mum, Mum! Watch! He's talking, and it's not working!'

We watched as our guide started talking into the microphone and giggled at his confusion when he realised nothing was coming out. Eventually—sadly—he and the driver figured it out, and we all had a laugh together before the screeching resumed. We continued along past Tibetan villages with colourful flags and temples, small villages and fields with grazing yaks, roaring rivers and snow-capped mountains as we got closer and closer to the Tibetan Plateau.

Our first stop was Huanglong Valley, where cascading travertine pools of blue water formed by calcite deposits flowed slowly down the mountain. With an elevation of 3600 metres, the air was thin. We could feel it as soon as we got out of the bus, but I had no idea that I needed to take this seriously. As usual, I just assumed it was something we could push through.

Hiking up the mountain to try to reach the multi-level blue pools within two hours was a tough ask, and only when Emmie's lips started turning blue and we both had headaches did I realise that the locals carrying bottles of oxygen probably had the right idea.

'Okay, Emmie, abort mission,' I puffed.

We slowly started back down the wooden pathways lined with forest, past beautiful pools of water, and I kicked myself for not taking the chairlift to the top and walking down. Why did I always have to choose the tough-person route? From now on, we would take the easy way if we wanted to. We were also busting to go to the loo, and there were none in sight.

'Mum, I need to go,' Emmie said desperately. 'Can I do a bush wee?'

'Bloody hell, Emmie, okay but be quick, alright?'

She squatted in the scrub by the side of the path, and I decided I may as well go, too.

'Emmie, remember the rules. If someone comes, just let me know immediately, okay? Don't let me get caught.' I had zero faith in her. I knew she would love it if I was spotted.

'Sure, Mum,' she promised and then, just as I squatted in the short scrub, she started yelling to draw attention. 'Excuse me. Do not come down here, my mum is doing a wee. I repeat, MY MUM IS DOING A WEE! Mum! *Hoot hoot*! Mum, it's your warning call. Someone is coming.'

It was panic stations, with my pants around my ankles.

'Mum, someone really is coming,' she yelled. 'Put your pants on.'

'Emmie, stop them!'

Emmie ran off to stop the couple from getting any closer (she was probably hurrying them up so they would catch me out), and I pulled myself together and stood up to say hello.

'Oh, Mum, these are my new friends, I was just talking to them while you did your wee.' She was laughing hard and trying to be serious, pretending she was being helpful rather than trying to embarrass me.

'*Ni hao*, how are you?' I asked, and we smiled awkwardly at each other.

'She is so cute!' they said.

I looked at Emmie with eyebrows raised and a big smile. 'You think so?'

That evening, we watched a traditional Tibetan music and dance performance and slept in a manky hotel that didn't supply linen or towels. While our friends distracted the man guarding the front desk, we relieved the storeroom of enough supplies to make our beds and dry ourselves off after a shower, even though we were using tiny hand towels. It reminded me of the old backpacker days. The next morning, we were off bright and early to Jiuzhaigou National Park for a full day of exploring. Natta braided Emmie's hair in the back of the bus, and we tried to figure out where we would go. The park is huge and there were more than 100 alpine lakes and rivers to see, plus waterfalls and pristine forest. We only had one day to see as much as we could and I had absolutely no information, so I decided that we would follow the gang. Luckily, national parks in China are incredibly well-organised. They have to be; the Chinese love exploring their own awesome country, and with a population well over one billion, that's a lot of domestic tourists. Jiuzhaigou has modern pathways, lots of bins and notices to not litter, a well-organised shuttle bus route, and maps and information in Chinese and English so everyone can experience this incredible nature.

We walked around vibrant lakes so clear that we could see all the way to the deep bottom, and majestic waterfalls forcefully flowing only metres away from us as we traipsed along wooden pathways through the forest. China is home to some of the most pristine, untouched nature in the world, and seeing this little part of it made me think of how much more beauty is out there to discover, something I find inspiring and scary at the same time. I desperately want to see it all but I know I never will, and even if I could, I would always want more. I will never be satisfied, no matter how much of this incredible planet I get to explore.

We continued our love affair with China, booking a sixteen-hour overnight train ride from Chengdu to Xi'an. There's something special about train travel in China. We both find it such an adventure but also so soothing and relaxing. We read, eat, play cards and drop off to sleep to the sounds and movement of the train as we speed through the Chinese countryside. At least we do when I get the bookings right, not when I book us into a stinky third-class carriage next to a toilet and smoking room.

We boarded our train to Xi'an, dragging our packs up the big steps and setting off down the walkway searching for our compartment and our seats, which we assumed we would turn into beds later on. We were pretty happy to get onboard, especially since it was a Chinese holiday when everything becomes very crowded, and we'd been lucky to get tickets at all. I started to suspect something was amiss when the carriage just didn't seem, well … fresh. It was a little manky and stale, and when we found our compartment, oh … there were no seats, just two long bunk beds attached to each wall of the tiny compartment, with a man sitting on one of the lower ones. There was no door, so there was no privacy, but I thought that was safer since we were sharing with a stranger.

'Ni hao!' We said hello and then got down to business. 'Righto then, Emmie. I guess the top two are ours,' I said.

I heaved our bags up onto our beds and we threw the daypacks up, too, pushing them down to the ends where our feet would be. Next, we unrolled our sleeping sheets over the provided sheets and pillows and we climbed up. That's when I discovered that the beds were so close to the ceiling, I couldn't sit up. I would have to lie in my coffin bed for the entire journey with the ceiling less than a metre from my face, the toilet and cigarette stench wafting past.

'Pick a number,' yelled Emmie as she shoved her paper chatterbox across the gap and into my face.

'Three.'

'Pick a colour.'

'Blue.'

'Pick another number.'

'Seven.'

'And your fortune iiiissss? Mum! Your fortune is you will be stuck lying down on a stinky train for *seventeen hours*! How do you feel about that?'

Ha. Leave it to Emmie to make me laugh. It wasn't so bad. I comfort-ate most of our snacks and felt a little better. We were tired, and I had enough space to hold a book in front of my face. We played games and the stale air cleared as soon as we started moving towards Xi'an. And when the carriage lights were turned off at 11.00 pm, everyone went to bed. Hilarious! No one mucked up or made noise at all. We had a good time on that train—the little blips can make everything more fun.

In Xi'an, we mapped our route to the Terracotta Army on the public transport bus and found it easily. The Terracotta Army was discovered by farmers in 1974, a kind of ghost army buried in pits to protect the first Emperor of China, Qin Shi Huang, in the afterlife. There are three pits with more than 8000 soldiers, 130 chariots with 520 horses and 150 cavalry horses, all made from terracotta. Historians reckon that 700,000 people worked on preparing the tomb for the emperor, who was buried in 210 BC. It was an incredible sight, rows and rows of ancient terracotta statues standing in the earth, striking and menacing, although we'd had to walk through a fast-food mecca of Maccas and Starbucks to get there.

Our next adventure was always going to be a highlight—we were going camping on the Great Wall of China. Emmie was super invested because this had been her idea. We had researched together and discovered a small number of groups offering over-night camping trips. We found Fred and Heidi's ChinaHiking company online, and the husband-and-wife team seemed lovely. Fred is from Belgium and Heidi is from Inner Mongolia, and they run their awesome little business themselves, leading small groups of tourists up to deserted parts of the wall to sleep in watchtowers and experience its magic under the stars.

Involving Emmie in working out where we would visit, how long we would stay and even just in our day-to-day decisions was important to both of us. We stopped when Emmie wanted to, visited countries and places she was interested in, and I made sure I valued her suggestions. I considered her my travel partner, and her ideas were just as valuable as mine (although I had the last say when needed). She has always been pretty cluey and mature for her age. I guess that's just her, but also the result of being in a single-parent home, where we talk a lot one-on-one and I ask her for her opinion all the time.

The following morning, we packed up all our gear and took a local train to the outskirts of Beijing, where we met Heidi and the six other people in our group. After a couple of hours on a minibus, we arrived at a small village where we ate a delicious green bean, tofu and chicken curry lunch at a local home before putting our hiking backpacks on and starting the climb.

'Oh my gosh, Mum, I can't believe we are here! I can't believe we are climbing up!' Emmie was raring to go and couldn't wait to start.

We were climbing in a deserted area at Jiankou, up a steep, scrubby mountain to an original and wild section of the wall, then to the Jade Watchtower, where we would camp for the night. There were no tourist groups and bobsleds here. This was the authentic wall. We'd sleep in the tents we were carrying before hiking back down the mountain after breakfast the following day. We were in hiking boots, shorts and t-shirts, and we both had caps as the sun was hot and strong.

'We are on a huge mission,' announced Emmie. 'We will make it to the top of this Great Wall of China, and together we will defeat the Huns!'

'Lead the way, Emmie!' I cried, and she did, scurrying up the mountainside with me behind her, legs burning and feeling fabulous. We were on a mission, just like Emmie said, and it felt wonderful.

The hike was challenging—a solid four hours of climbing up the side of the mountain. Emmie was so into it, maybe because she knew there was something amazing at the end for us. She became very competitive and desperately wanted to be the first of our group to reach the top, which was fine for her—she didn't have the backpack on her back and daypack on her front! She had started off with a daypack, but it was a little tough for her so I carried it. She climbed on ahead, over rocks and big boulders, only having the occasional whinge when long grass and sticks scratched her legs.

We sang songs and talked about what we'd loved doing so far on our trip. Emmie wondered when she would get to eat more *xiao long bao,* and we giggled and enjoyed our time together. It was so precious to share these moments with Emmie, and that we were climbing the Great Wall of China together kind of blanked out my mind; it was hard to comprehend this was actually happening. My legs ached as we climbed steep, dusty paths, over boulders with bugs and birds flapping around us, but we pushed on, and after hours of climbing up that rough, rocky path, we reached the wall.

'Mum, I think we're here,' Emmie yelled. 'I can see some bricks.'

At first, it was just a few random bricks covered with crawling grass, then it was piles of bricks and finally we hoisted ourselves onto the wild original wall built way back in the 1300s during the Ming Dynasty. We had done this together—this overwhelming, challenging adventure. It will live with me forever. At that moment, I truly felt like we could do anything.

'I can't believe we made it, Emmie!' This was such an achieve-ment for the two of us, and I was so proud of her. We had hiked up to the Great Wall of China, and we were going to sleep here! We high-fived and had a cuddle and then started walking along the uneven, falling-apart wall, picking our way across the ancient bricks and places where workers and soldiers had trod centuries before. It was tough going as we followed the wall's curved spine, climbing up and over the bricks and the creeping plants that kept the majestic wall wild and living. Finally, we made it to the 650-year-old Jade Watchtower, where we would be staying the night.

It's hard to describe that feeling of being on the wall. The atmosphere was heavy and other-worldly. I had constant goosebumps and—a feeling? a vibe?—a sense of *something*. There was an essence, an electricity, maybe the energy of the spirits of the hundreds of thousands of people who died building it, the souls of the wall. Emmie could feel it, too. It was emotional, thick.

Emmie and I wanted to sleep on top of the watchtower, looking out over the wall. We climbed the steep steps and found a broken, weed-covered space with a spectacular view of the wall weaving across the mountains and down into the valleys, perfect for spotting approaching enemies. We pitched our tent, spread out our sleeping bags and sat on the wall, holding hands as the sun set and our spines tingled.

Heidi cooked dinner in a little frypan over an open fire, and we ate rice and vegies and toasted marshmallows. She told stories of the wall: how a million workers built all 21,000 kilometres of it by hand, using cement made out of rice and dirt to stick the bricks together. She told us about the guards on the watchtower who spent their days alone, watching for approaching enemies, and how they burned dried wolf poo to send smoke signals to other guards along the wall. Everything had a purpose out here.

It was dark and quiet as we climbed into our sleeping bags and lay in the silence of the still night, absorbing the atmosphere under the stars as gigantic bugs buzzed around and crashed into the tent.

'Sweet dreams, Mummy, on the Great Wall of China,' said Emmie.

I woke up early and crept out to wait for the sun to rise over the wall. Through the misty white fog I could see the wall, winding like a ribbon through the forest. I sat in silence, feeling the weight of the wall in my heart. Emmie joined me, and in the hazy golden light we acknowledged the magnificence of the wall and the sacrifice of those who built it. It was a perfect moment.

Soon it was time to go. We packed up our tent, had a cup of tea and noodles for breakfast and made our way back down the mountain, so sad to leave it all behind.

'Wasn't that just amazing, Emmie?' I sighed, still a little overwhelmed.

'Mum, I loved it. It was the best,' she smiled.

This adventure was humbling. It was bigger than us. It was a first-time experience for both of us, and to do it together gave us a heartfelt memory to share and never forget.

⌣

Back in the city, we spent two nights in absolute luxury at the Shangri-La Beijing, arriving dirty and smelly into the sparkling lobby and rushing to our room to shower. We scoffed Peking Duck in the Shang Palace restaurant, wandered the gorgeous gardens and fed the koi in the hotel ponds. It was a beautiful stay. My only mistake was letting the hotel book me a car to the airport when I knew I could grab one on the street. We'd had no trouble with taxis so far, but this one would be a problem.

'It will cost 100 yuan,' the receptionist told us (about $25) and I agreed, even though I felt uneasy and it went against my gut. I didn't want to seem cheap while I was in this gorgeous hotel, so the next day, we set off in a fancy car costing us a little more money than a street car, but a lot of my pride.

We should have left earlier. There was so much traffic, and I was freaking out about missing our flight. We were off to Bangkok to meet my mum, and I was even more stressed about getting to the airport on time than usual. The driver did not speak a word of English, so I was miming my desperation but there wasn't much he could do. We were in a sea of traffic, with cars stuck in front of us, behind us and by our side. I was sure we were going to miss the plane. It was my nightmare come true. I was anxious and frustrated, and that made Emmie more chatty and jokey as she messed around while I counted the seconds rushing past. 'Mum, Mum, are you worried? What will you do if you miss the flight? Where will we stay?'

We finally made it through the traffic and pulled up at the airport. Emmie and I grabbed our bags out of the car, I paid the driver the 100 yuan and we set off for the departure doors. But the driver followed us, looking at the notes, and then started gesturing for more.

'No, it was a hundred, right?' I said. He shook his head. He wanted more money.

Had I not been so anxious, I probably would have realised that all he wanted was another few dollars and decided to leave my battle for another day. Instead, I was immediately angry and not in the mood to be ripped off. My backpacking genes kicked in.

'No,' I said. 'One hundred!' And I kept walking towards the entrance. He stood in front of me, up against my body so I couldn't really move. I should have paid the money then, but what I did instead was press forward. I don't know where I thought I would get with this, and I didn't care who was looking. At that moment of stress, this driver would *not* get the best of me. I didn't yet realise that by me behaving like this, he already had. So, with Emmie whacking him with her teddy bear and me pushing forward, we made our way through the departures doors, down the big main ramp and into the check-in area. People were staring, and I knew it. We must have been a sight. I mean, how absolutely ridiculous! But I was determined that I wouldn't be taken advantage of.

Eventually, a security guard came over to see what the fuss was. I couldn't plead my case due to the language barrier, and he spoke to the driver and made me pay the extra money. What could I do? I knew I wouldn't get anywhere if I argued, but I wasn't happy about it. We raced to the check-in counter and just made it to the flight. Thai Airways was so kind and escorted us all the way to the plane—and I found time to grab a coffee on the way.

Once I had calmed down, I was so embarrassed. That was not good behaviour, especially for Emmie to see. And what if someone had filmed us? I'd lost my mind. Emmie was okay and we had a giggle about her and the teddy, but I'll never completely laugh at it because, regardless of the circumstances, it was bad conduct on my part and created unnecessary worry for her.

'My mummy, the dragon,' said Emmie. 'We are the Dragon Team.'

What I learned from this was to pick my battles and accept that we would be ripped off once in a while. Should I let that bother me and watch every cent and travel with a cynical and suspicious attitude, or just accept that people who need money or see me as a walking wallet would sometimes try to get a little more from us, and just roll with it? A few dollars was not worth the drama, especially in countries where I didn't speak the language and didn't have any allies. From then on, I just accepted that wherever we were, I would probably get ripped off in one way or another, and it would probably cost me a few dollars. Big deal. To travel suspiciously would close us off to opportunities and chances to get to know local people. It just wasn't worth it. And so ended our first visit to one of our favourite countries. A little drama, a little embarrassment, but an important new way of thinking.

CHAPTER 9

Please don't ride elephants

Emmie spotted my mum at Bangkok airport and ran to her through the crowd. I could see Mum's face crumple as she started crying and scooped Emmie up in a huge hug. Family reunions are always so emotional, and it was great to be with Mum again, especially in Bangkok, a chaotic, energetic city that I loved. We finished our tears and jumped into a taxi to our hotel, the beautiful riverside Chatrium, where Mum delightedly revealed the contents of her bag one precious item at a time. There were bottles of my favourite Evans & Tate Classic Dry White, a sports bra, deodorant (Yay! No more rubbing limes under my arms!), tweezers, multivitamins, face cream, OOFOS thongs and some Lego for Emmie.

'Nanny, I'm so happy you're here to play with me,' Emmie said. 'Can we just swim and build Lego for a while?'

We were hungry, and I couldn't wait to get into the Bangkok street food—I reckon it's the best in all of Asia—so we left the hotel for a wander. We passed locals making salads and cooking noodles, vegetables, fried chicken and skewers of squid, prawns and sausage at carts on the side of the road. There were street-side stalls displaying tropical fruit, coconuts, fresh juices and mango rice, with people chopping, mixing, cooking and serving fresh, delicious dishes. Locals wheeled their food stalls around—mobility was king here. I watched a man take a portable barbecue from the back of his bike and set up a roadside pork stand, searing the meat he pulled out from under his seat. Yes, of course I tried it—and it was good.

We jumped right into Bangkok and did everything we could. We made green curry and spring rolls at a Thai cooking class, took a ferry along the Chao Phraya River to the Temple of the Reclining Buddha, learned to fold lotuses at the flower markets for temple offerings, and went to Wat Arun, with its intricate tiling and spires reaching to the sky. We gave alms to the monks at sunrise, visited museums and shopping centres, and Emmie had a few hours at KidZania, a family entertainment centre, where she role-played having adult jobs but still didn't learn how to pack her bag.

We had to see one of Bangkok's signature performances, the Calypso Cabaret at the Asiatique, which is famous for its fabulous choreography. Emmie had been fascinated with the beautiful *kathoey* (transgender) performers since that wonderfully random show at the Bohol reptile park and couldn't wait to see it. She danced in her seat as she eyed off the elaborate costumes, the choreography and detailed sets, and soaked up the energy that radiated from the stage.

'I love the dresses, Mum. I love the designs. The ladies are beautiful!' she said.

See you later, Sydney!
The start of our adventure.

*Emmie snorkelling in
Coron in the Philippines
– we carried our masks
and snorkels with us, and
jumped into the ocean
wherever we could.*

*Rope swinging into
Cambugahay Falls in
Siquijor, the Philippines.*

We don't count flights or countries, just happy times.

Being with Emmie made me braver and stronger. I love that she convinced me to do things I didn't want to.

Looking out to Taipei 101 from Elephant Mountain in Taiwan.

The stunning Masjid Bandaraya in Kota Kinabalu, Malaysian Borneo.

Spotting orangutans at Sepilok, Malaysian Borneo.

Lazy days at Pulau Rawa, Malaysia.

Malaysia's Kuala Lumpur is one of our favourite cities.

China is Emmie's favourite country — for people, nature and xiao long bao.

The opening of Disneyland Shanghai, China.

Bamboo rafting down the Yulong River in Yangshuo, China.

Spending the night on the Great Wall of China was one of the best things we did on our trip.

Enjoying the view from the Great Wall of China before setting up our tent on top of a watchtower.

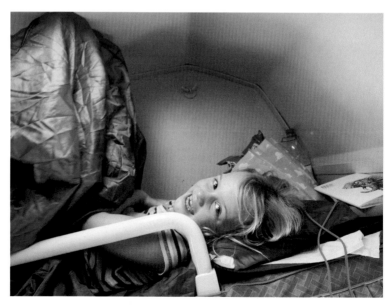

The overnight train from Chengdu to Xi'an, China.

Transport in Koh Lipe, Thailand.

Wat Sri Suphan in Chiang Mai, Thailand.

I always say yes now when people offer to take our photo – it's why we have this pic from Paris, France that I love. #mumsinphotos

The stunning Kölner Dom (Cologne Cathedral), in Germany.

Emmie can sleep anywhere now!

We loved our afternoons in Vietnam's Hội An, riding our bike and wandering through the rice paddies.

Receiving a blessing at Angkor Wat, Cambodia.

Riding the bamboo railway in Battambang, Cambodia.

Weaving our way through the Tonlé Sap on the way to Battamabang, Cambodia.

Our first year of travel went so quickly – it was the best time of my life.

Beautiful Sambo is one of the many rescued elephants at the Elephant Valley Project in Cambodia.

Donating blood at Cambodia's Angkor Hospital for Children.

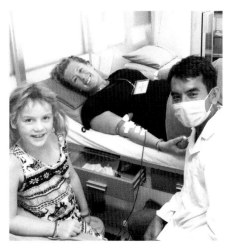

Learning to surf in Sri Lanka's Hiriketiya with Madhu, a local surf teacher.

We have special memories of sitting in Sri Lanka's blue train doorways.

Heartbroken Emmie with a chained elephant.

The Maldives were just as stunning as we thought they would be.

The famously busy Shibuya crossing in Tokyo, Japan.

Exploring little nests in Bedugul in Bali, Indonesia.

The famous Yellow Bridge in Nusa Lembongan, Indonesia.

We all sat and watched, enthralled by the beauty and talent of the performers, and angry when we heard men in the audience nearby heckling them.

'That's not nice, Mum, is it?' Emmie said.

I agreed, but I stopped myself from telling them to be quiet. 'Emmie, you're always going to have people who aren't open-minded, or disagree with what you're doing. Ignore them and focus on the good people. There's more of them anyway.'

The next day, we boarded our flight to Chiang Mai in northern Thailand. We could have taken the train, but it was cheaper to fly with the local carrier, Thai Smile. Somehow, Emmie and I had been upgraded to business class, where we were handed a drink on arrival as my mum trudged down the back.

'Nanny, we have a welcome drink! Did you get a welcome drink?' Emmie yelled, waving her little cup of orange juice in the air. I offered to swap seats with Mum, but she needed a break from us, and I didn't blame her; we are exhausting. The joy of an upgrade wasn't wasted on me, though, and we drank our welcome drinks and took off into the sky.

'And here we go,' we said. We hadn't missed a take-off or landing yet.

Checking into our guesthouse at Chiang Mai, we were asked for our passports, as usual. That was the moment I remembered that I'd put them in the seat pocket on the plane for just a minute while I drank my welcome drink ... and left them there.

'Okay, no problem! Mum, you stay here with Emmie, and I'll go back.' My crisis-management background put me straight into operational mode: solve the problem, there's no time for emotion! I had to get to the airport quickly, as the plane would be turning around to fly back to Bangkok. I jumped into a car and rushed back to the quiet little airport, where I found the Thai Airways office. The manager made a couple of phone calls, and after a few minutes of anticipation, *voila*! The passports were delivered to the office— the staff had found them in the seat pocket. Another happy ending.

We had a bad habit of leaving things on planes. Emmie left her iPad in the seat pocket four times. Three of those times it was returned, but the last time, in transit in Vietnam, it disappeared. She was very lucky it was mostly covered by insurance.

Chiang Mai is an ancient city, the historical capital of the Lanna Kingdom, founded more than 800 years ago. It's surrounded by misty mountains and split by the Ping River, a tributary of the Chao Phraya River that flows through Bangkok.

We settled in straight away and loved hailing communal *songthaew* trucks and walking the streets. We stopped at some of the 300 Buddhist *wats* (temples), crossed ancient moats and passed through the old town's city walls, finding a huge green park where Emmie slack-lined with a bunch of twenty-something digital nomads. Chiang Mai is a popular place for travellers to stop and rest and work, and it crossed my mind that it would be a good spot for us to stay for a while.

We decided to visit an elephant sanctuary, not knowing much about elephant tourism and why—or if—sanctuaries were necessary. We chose what we thought was an ethical operation, thinking we could spend time with the elephants and give them love.

The day before we were to visit the sanctuary, we set out to Mae Wang to go bamboo rafting. On the way, our driver pulled off the road and into a clearing, where four elephants with chains around their legs were standing in the dirt.

'Now you can ride elephants,' he said.

Oh, no. This was not for us. We looked at the majestic, beautiful animals swaying in the heat with heavy chains around their legs, severely limiting their movement. Their skin was mottled, they had a small pile of thin, dry branches to eat, and they were obviously not where they should be. We looked at each other in horror.

'No, thank you, no. This is very cruel, and we won't be riding elephants,' I told him, shaking my head.

'What was he thinking?' Mum asked me. 'This is awful.' She put her arm around Emmie.

'These poor elephants,' Emmie sobbed. 'I want to feed them, can I give them some food?' She grabbed some banana leaves from a nearby pile and dragged them over to where the elephants were standing.

We watched as an elephant struggled to climb a dirt path with two heavy Western tourists sitting on a wooden throne on its back, and we looked down into the river where people were bathing elephants. They were mostly posing, though, standing on the elephants' trunks and backs, not caring about the pain they were causing. It was heartbreaking, and we could do nothing to stop it. We walked back to the chained elephants, and Emmie pulled more leaves over to them, desperate to help.

'Here you are, beautiful elephants,' she said softly, tears in her eyes. 'I'm so sorry.'

That night we researched elephant tourism and learned about the brutal cruelty used to break the elephants' spirits so they could be ridden. We learned how weak their backs are and how every step with a person on them causes immense pain, how they are separated from their herd and aren't able to forage and bellow and enjoy life in the wild. The industry is heartbreaking. It was something Emmie grew very passionate about, becoming upset whenever we saw elephants in camps or being chained up on the side of the road, and sharing information wherever she could. It was even worse seeing people riding them. It was just so wrong.

Still, the next day we set out to the elephant sanctuary, thinking we were doing the right thing, supporting rescued elephants. In retrospect, I think our motives were mostly selfish. Like many people, we were fascinated by these gorgeous creatures, and we wanted to feed them and help them, but really, we wanted to visit for us, and what we could get out of it. Time with cute elephants and photos.

Now, when I think back, I have more clarity. While we might want to show our love for elephants by hugging them, feeding them and washing them—the programs most sanctuaries offer tourists—I'm sure the elephants don't want our hugs, or to be paraded in front of a bunch of tourists. It's scary for them. Elephants want to be in the jungle, wild and free, where they can move around, forage and rumble and be with their elephant community. And how satisfying are likes and comments on an Instagram elephant photo if it's based in cruelty, no matter how you try to justify it? I can tell you: not very. And I know, because I posted some before I realised this.

We were told that the sanctuary we visited rescued their elephants from camps where they were used for rides, and that these elephants couldn't be released into the wild because there was not enough jungle for them to forage in. The staff seemed knowledgeable and explained that the elephants would eat crops and farmers would then attack the elephants, so they needed to be in the sanctuary where they had a nice life, even if they did have to hang with tourists every day.

I now feel like we didn't really question anything because we wanted that experience, so we chose to believe whatever we needed to. I'm not an expert, though. If the elephants are well cared for, and the local community is earning money, who am I to judge? Especially if I can't offer an alternative and don't know enough about it all. It's a tough one. What I'd suggest is to do a lot of research before visiting a sanctuary, and to leave your phone or camera behind.

And please don't ride elephants.

⌣

Having Mum with us was so much fun, but she worried that her snoring would keep us awake at night. Emmie and I returned to our room at the Maraya Hotel to find she that had set up a new bed for herself, inside the shower.

'Mum, this is ridiculous, you can't sleep in the shower!' I laughed at her, but she was adamant that she had worked it all out.

'After everyone has had a shower, I just dry it off, pull the mattress and pillows in and shut the door. It's like an overnight cryogenic chamber,' she told me.

'Mum, that is crazy. We don't mind if you snore. And you're not a frozen body!'

She put her foot down and slept in the shower for the rest of our time in Chiang Mai. Utterly hilarious. Mums, huh?

A few days later, I received an email from Thai Airways, who said they'd been following our travels on Instagram and would like to work with us. This was such an amazing and unexpected offer—to work with one of the best airlines in the world! Thai Airways very generously wanted to fly us return to Sydney so we could test out their economy class with kids. We weren't keen on going back home yet, but I wondered if they might fly us to Paris instead? I almost wasn't going to ask, but I remembered my friend Simone's favourite saying: if you don't ask, you don't get. Paris was kind of the same distance away from Thailand as Sydney, and it was completely different to what we'd done so far. We wouldn't have gone there if we hadn't had this opportunity, but why not? So, I asked, and Thai Airways very kindly agreed. We were going to Paris!

It was a big day when I started finding my voice and feeling like we were valuable enough to be able to ask for things. At the time, I wasn't confident and underestimated the benefits and results we could bring to brands and partners. I'm still working on that, and I think it's a struggle that most women face, especially if we've been told for years that we shouldn't think highly of ourselves. We need to love ourselves more, that's for sure, and I teach Emmie this, too.

'Emmie, guess what?' I yelled when I received the email. 'We're going to Paris!'

'Oh, Mummy, they said yes? Can we climb the Eiffel Tower?'

'Of course we can, ladybug! That's at the top of our list. And we can do whatever we like. Let's practise our French to be polite.'

Emmie loves tall buildings. She adored Taipei 101 in Taiwan and obsessed over the Shanghai Tower in China, but she wanted to see the Eiffel Tower most of all. I couldn't think of anything better than Paris with Emmie. I'd promised her we could go on her sixteenth birthday, but it was going to happen ten years earlier, lucky girl. I started researching where else to go in Europe, but planning ahead still annoyed me. I wanted to enjoy where I was, not be sitting somewhere amazing and researching, reading about and planning for somewhere else. We decided to spend ten days in Paris and pop over to London to visit Jacqui, who, by coincidence, would be in town. Then we would go to Cologne to meet up with Viktoria, our beautiful au pair, before heading back to Thailand.

We were so happy in Asia. We loved the people, the different cultures and the kindness. We loved the focus on family and how people lived and worked together and seemed to really care for each other. Exploring the streets of Paris would be a totally different adventure—one that we were so excited for—but we were still very much in love with Asia. I always feel so safe there and, when Paris was targeted by terrorists, I was a little hesitant to go.

I generally don't worry about these things, but it was playing on my mind because I seem to have a knack for being near drama. My first backpacking trip with Jacqui had been full of near misses, and at the end of our travels, I was stuck in a hostel in Cairo with a ringworm infection in my arm and the grumblings of appendicitis in my belly. There'd been terrorist attacks, and I couldn't get home. In previous weeks, a tourist bus had been bombed at the Cairo Museum, and a few days after we visited Hatshepsut Temple in Luxor, terrorists ambushed and killed 62 tourists. We were so lucky with our timing and felt that strange *Sliding Doors* kind of feeling. It had been very close. Back in the day, you needed to confirm your seat a few days before your flight, and when I'd gone into the Qantas office in Cairo, I was told I no longer had one. My seat, booked and paid for more than ten months earlier, had been given to someone else in the clamour of tourists trying to get out of the country.

'All the tourists are leaving,' the airline representative told me. 'You don't have a seat anymore. Come back in two months.'

Jacqui was lucky and still had her flight to London, but I was stuck. Every transport option out of the country was full, and I needed help. There was no internet, so I was on the phone to my insurance company reverse-charges at the telephone exchange every day, trying to get out. A few days after I was supposed to leave, they said they were pretty sure they had me on a flight and to head to the airport. I jumped on a bus all alone with my backpack and crossed my fingers, not feeling very confident at all. At the airport, I sat on a tiny piece of floor in the huge departures hall crammed with thousands of other people. Some had been waiting there for days, sleeping on the ground, desperate to get out. After waiting for a few hours, my name was called—I was on the flight home! As I picked my way across the crowded floor to the check-in counter, people stared jealously and asked me how I did it. I knew that the only reason I had a seat on the flight was because of my travel insurance. I was extra lucky, as two days after I arrived home, I was rushed to hospital for an emergency appendectomy.

Now I had a big decision to make about Paris. It wasn't just me this time; I had Emmie to look after. I asked my friends at home— my travel brains trust—for advice and after talking it through, I decided we would go. We would be careful and alert, and we would have a great time.

Our time in Thailand was up for now, so we flew back to Bangkok, said goodbye to Mum at the airport and took the red-eye to Paris. We arrived early in the morning at Charles de Gaulle Airport, bumbled through immigration and customs, and found the airport train to the city. We then took the metro to Saint-Paul and popped up on the main drag in Le Marais, with only a short walk to our hotel. I'd taken the advice of my friend Bryce, who'd lived in Paris for many years, and booked into the Hôtel Jeanne d'Arc. It was a small hotel on a cobblestone street right behind the Place Sainte-Catherine courtyard, a few steps from the Place des Vosges park and walking distance from almost everything.

It was early and our room wasn't ready, so we decided to walk the streets, changing in the small toilet at reception and trying to freshen up before we left the hotel. Getting outdoors would be good for us; I reckon it's the best way to beat jet lag. We grabbed a drink and a croissant each from the breakfast room and walked into the morning light, ready to explore this beautiful city. *Paris, here we are!*

Holding hands, we wandered down the Rue de Rivoli, surrounded by the morning bustle of a city waking up as we gazed up at the blue sky and the beautiful ornate buildings. We turned onto Rue Saint-Paul, drawn towards the enchanting Seine, the river at the heart of Paris.

'I can't believe we're in Paris!' we repeated to each other.

'I love you, Mum, thank you so, so much, Mum! We're in Paris!' Emmie squeezed my hand and jumped around with so much energy it surprised me. We'd just come off our overnight flight and had little sleep. It didn't matter, she was so happy to be here.

We felt so alive in the morning sun in Paris. We strolled past a heavy police detail, which was a bit unsettling but reassuring. Wandering along the riverside, we spotted deck chairs on the banks and huge patches of sand for games of pétanque. Emmie stopped to watch a group of adults throwing silver boules in turn, trying to get their pairs closest to a small wooden jack nestled in the sand.

'*Bonjour,*' she yelled out, waving. The players seemed very serious about their game but surprisingly, heart-soaringly, they kindly started talking to Emmie.

'*Bonjour!*' they waved back. '*Parlez-vous français?*'

'Non, je parle français une petite et très mal,' I replied, drawing on my Year 10 French and hoping it made sense.

'Oh, that's okay,' said one of the ladies. 'Two of us are from America, so we can talk in English. I'm Sam. Would you like to join us for a game?'

'Can we, Mummy? Is it okay?'

Of course it was! I got a bit teary at the kindness of these strangers as we walked over to join them.

'Hello, welcome,' said Sam with a smile as she introduced us to everyone. 'We're down a person today, so it's great to have you here. Do you know how to play?'

The pétanque players were three French men and the two ex-pat American women who'd been meeting up to play by the river for eight years. They showed us how to play, and we spent an hour slowly taking turns, throwing then walking to collect our balls and chatting as the sun rose higher in the sky and Paris sparkled even more for us.

Isn't it strange to feel such a sense of belonging in places so far away from home? To feel so cared for by strangers? I will never forget our morning on the Seine with these lovely, kind people who let us into their lives and made our day so special. Most importantly for me, they made Emmie so happy. I watched as they bent over to talk to her and patiently show her how to hold the silver boules, and how to throw them softly to land near the jack. The night before, we'd been in noisy, chaotic, bustling Bangkok, and now we were on the banks of the Seine in Paris, playing pétanque with a bunch of new friends. All along our travels, little whims delivered pockets of magic. These were the moments that made me happiest.

After an hour or so, we said goodbye and continued exploring, crossing the Pont d'Arcole, where a passing lady kindly offered to take our photo. It's one of the few we have together in Paris because back then I lacked the confidence to get in photos, and would always refuse offers from people to photograph us together. When we got home, I could hardly believe it—there were entire countries where we'd spent months, and there was no photographic evidence that I'd been there at all. There were lots of photos of Emmie and scenery, and not one of me. I'd made myself invisible. What would happen when Emmie was older and went looking for photos with me on all our travels? What if she couldn't find any? I searched and searched and thankfully found enough of the two of us, butit made me realise that because of my insecurity about how I looked, I'd often denied Emmie precious memories. Who cares how I looked! Emmie was more important to me.

Later, I would share my thoughts on Instagram and ask if other mums felt the same. They did, and it was so sad. Mums are not in photos for so many reasons, and some had heartbreaking stories of looking for photos of their mums and not finding any. I created the hashtag #mumsinphotos and encouraged everyone to get into the pictures with their kids, and to use the hashtag when they shared their photos. I am in so, so many photos now, and I never say no when people offer to take our photo. I love looking at everyone's photos and at the photo of the two us in Paris, seeing the joy on our faces. I'm so glad I said yes.

We wandered past the Notre-Dame de Paris Cathedral, surprised at the crowds already queuing to visit, with so many tourists and their guides, coloured flags waving in the breeze blowing across the courtyard. When I had been in Paris years before, I had walked into Notre-Dame on spec one day, joining Mass as the choir sang and the sun shone through the stained-glass windows. There was no chance of that right now. We continued along little streets, into a patisserie for more croissants, *pains au chocolat* and coffee before crossing the Seine again, walking past the fountains of the Place des Vosges back to our hotel. We could check in now and found we had been upgraded to a lovely room with a double and a single bed, a chair and table, and French windows that opened out over the street below, through which Emmie would later sail paper planes with love notes on them. And then we slept.

The next day, we took the bus from Rue de Rivoli to the Eiffel Tower, spotting it in the distance as we drew closer.

'I see it, I see it, Mum,' Emmie shouted, bouncing on her seat. We walked through the Champ de Mars and stopped for photos in front of the tower, below the tower and everywhere around the tower, before getting our tickets and taking the lift to the top. I'd climbed it before; there was no need to do that again. We looked out over Paris, spotting landmarks and looking up, down, around and all over the city. It was surreal, like a disconnect in my brain. Yet another one of our dreams come true.

We walked to the Trocadéro, and Emmie rode the carousel. We listened to buskers, saw the scammers try to swindle tourists with their card tricks, and watched the sun set and the tower light up, twinkling and gold. We visited the Musée National Picasso—Emmie's favourite—and the Musée de l'Orangerie—mine—for the magnificent, breathtaking Monet watercolours. We took the stairs to Montmartre in the early morning and wandered around the markets. Emmie had a caricature drawn by one of the artists who roamed the courtyard, and we explored the Sacré-Cœur Basilica, climbing to the top through musty passageways for another stunning view of Paris.

That afternoon, I had a message from one of my closest friends, Todd. 'Dahling, I heard you were in Paris. I'm coming. Where are you staying?'

It was just like Todd to swoop in and bring some extra sparkles and glitter to our Paris trip. He is hilarious, so much fun and such a beautiful, caring person. He makes me smile and laugh the whole time I'm around him, and he makes me feel so good about myself. Of course, being a gay American, he is very good-looking, rich, fit and super smart (at least, I know that's how he would want me to describe him—and it's all true!). We met at a charity ball during our peak party days in Sydney, when we would order bottles of champagne in harbour-side bars after work, party all weekend with a huge bunch of friends, drive to the beach in his black convertible, have weekends away in country towns and live our best city lives together with our big bunch of friends.

Some of my funniest, craziest memories are with Todd, like the time we went to a Darren Hayes concert, and Todd took off his underwear, wrote his phone number on them with my brand-new lipstick and threw them on stage—with a little too much force, as they hit Darren in the head. We snuck backstage to try to find the afterparty, or at least Darren's dressing room, but security kicked us out. Those were the days.

I couldn't believe that he was on his way to us from America. But first, Viktoria flew in from Cologne and met us at Disneyland Paris. We soaked up the magic of Disney and spent the day running from ride to ride. Back at the Hôtel Jeanne d'Arc, we discovered that Viktoria didn't have a booking—she had reserved a room at a hotel with the same name in Lourdes, and Todd had just booked the last room in the hotel—so she ended up sharing with us. Oh Viktoria, always so much fun.

When Emmie went to sleep, I sneaked out and bought a bottle of wine from a little cafe in the Place Sainte-Catherine, borrowed two glasses with a promise to return them the next day, and we sat in the bathroom and chatted and laughed for hours. I love travelling with Emmie, and while I don't get lonely, the bursts of time with friends that we have along the way are just super fun. Viktoria is hilarious, and I honestly felt like I was 21 again, sitting on top of the toilet in that tiny bathroom drinking red wine.

The next day, our fairy godfather Todd arrived with a case of Moët, and the fun times continued. It wasn't all champagne and red wine in Parisian courtyards, but there was quite a bit as we all explored together. We visited the Paris Museum of Modern Art and the Pompidou, and Todd treated us to a champagne breakfast at Ladurée on the Champs Elysées. We climbed the Arc de Triomphe and found the rooftop bar at Printemps where we ordered bottles of bubbles and gazed over the pastel-coloured rooftops to the Eiffel Tower. We ate dinner at a famous steakhouse, where Emmie fell asleep on my lap while Todd and I reminisced about the good old days in Sydney. It's definitely fun to have a gorgeous, rich and very generous friend! I felt so loved because Todd and Viktoria came to Paris. It touched my heart that they would make such an effort to see us.

After a few whirlwind days, our friends were gone and it was me and Emmie again, exploring together. Emmie found a random Barbie exhibition to visit, we spent hours in the Jardin du Luxembourg and explored the streets of Le Marais. We ate falafel and pastries and cheese and steak and *pommes frites*. We met up with Natta, who we'd met in China, and spent an afternoon with

Emmie's French au pair Coco (who coincidentally was living just around the corner from our hotel in Le Marais), at the Place des Vosges gardens sipping red wine under the trees while Emmie played. We explored and fell more in love with Paris, certain that our good fortune all started with the meeting with the pétanque players on our first day. We'd been travelling now for six months, and Paris was a beautiful mark in time. I'd had more happiness in the previous six months than I'd had in years. And we had so much more to come.

⌣

We raced over to visit Jacqui in London for a few days, then flew to Germany to stay with Viktoria and her family, eating generous German breakfasts at the family table and exploring the stunning city of Cologne, with its cobblestone streets, gorgeous architecture and low-rise buildings that always allowed us to see the sky. Then it was time to return to Asia on an overnight flight to Chiang Mai via Bangkok. We'd had a fabulous time on this unexpected leg of our adventure, but we were happy to be heading back to Asia, our true love.

Halfway through the flight, I realised that I had no idea about our connection. I hadn't paid much attention when I'd booked, and when I checked the tickets, I swore to myself. Our connection to Chiang Mai in Bangkok was so tight that we would be lucky to make it. Oh man, a race against the clock was coming up. I knew that if we missed the flight we could get another, no big deal. I just hated missing flights!

When we landed in Bangkok, we were pumped and ready to go. We bolted from the plane, sped through immigration, collected our backpack from the carousel, exited the international airport and ran to the domestic terminal to check in. I could hear Emmie laughing and cheering behind me, 'Go, Mummy, go' as I lumbered along, carrying everything. It was hilarious in its ridiculousness. I had the backpack on my back, two daypacks hanging off my arms, my handbag and a plastic bag full of all the junk Emmie had collected over the previous 24 hours. We just made it to the flight, arriving at the gate sweating and panting and laughing.

Together, we are definitely a great little team. I'd watched Emmie's skills develop over the past few months and had seen travelling bring out her confidence and independence. She was becoming so good with strategy and problem-solving, and was a huge help when things went wrong and we needed a fix. Her sense of humour was spot-on, too: she was so funny and had great timing. We had a lot of laughs on our travels. She was also great at staying in all kinds of accommodation, and although she does like a bit of fancy, she didn't bat an eye when we were staying basic. As long as we were together, everything was okay.

The plan was to stay in Chiang Mai and settle down for a few months. I was hoping to find a home-schooling group for Emmie so that she could do her schoolwork and I'd have time to work. I wasn't earning money yet, but I was starting to collaborate with brands, and it was important to me to do a good job. I'd also started to get some writing work from *Holidays with Kids* magazine in Australia, and I loved writing about our adventures, but it was hard to find time to do it. I didn't want to always be on my phone or computer, defeating the purpose of travelling, but if I could keep our money topped up, we'd have more options and could possibly travel longer.

On our third night, Emmie lost another wobbly tooth. 'It's my Thailand tooth, Mama,' she said. 'I've lost a tooth in Taiwan and Thailand now. I wonder how much I'll get?' She put the beautiful, shiny, white peg under her pillow with a handwritten note for the tooth fairy. 'Will the tooth fairy be able to find me, Mummy?'

'Of course she will, babe. She needs that tooth,' I assured her. When she woke up the next morning, she found some Thai baht under her pillow. Clever fairy.

I tried to settle into Chiang Mai, but I wasn't feeling the vibe. As so often happened, the universe sorted that out for me. A few nights after we arrived, I was supposed to be sleeping but playing on my phone instead when a message popped up from Kylie, a girl I went to school with. We weren't particularly close, but we'd been friendly and although I hadn't seen her since high school, here she was, saying hello.

Hey, I saw you were in Chiang Mai, she wrote. *My brother lives there, you should meet up.* Kylie was living in Hội An in Vietnam with her husband and two sons and absolutely loved it. By the time we had finished chatting, I'd decided that we'd join her for a month in Hội An. Kylie organised a guesthouse for Emmie and me, and put me in touch with the principal at Green Shoots International School. Two days later, I'd booked flights for the end of the week, organised our visas, enrolled Emmie into school and we were ready to go.

'Hey Emmie, guess what? We're moving on! We're going to spend some time in Vietnam.'

'Sure, okay, Mum. Sounds good.'

'And guess what? You're going to go to school! Yay!' I was so happy that Emmie was going to have a little bit of structured learning. She had been fighting me on the schoolwork for so long, it was time for her to head into the classroom.

'What Mum? Nooo, I don't want to,' she whinged at me, but I knew this could only be good.

'It's okay, babe, it's just for a month. You can see if you like it. I think it's going to be fun.'

I pulled out our map, and Emmie found Vietnam, then Hội An, and we learned how to say hello in Vietnamese. She didn't mind moving on, and I really needed this. The daily schoolwork battles with Emmie were making me lose my mind, and Distance Education had been emailing me about the lack of schoolwork we'd submitted. I had emailed them to explain how hard it was to carry all the blue folders, our teaching difficulties and that Emmie would be spending a month at international school, and could that please count for some of her schooling? Mr Brown came to my rescue again and arranged for Emmie to be credited for attending Green Shoots. We were off the hook, at least for a little while.

Later, I re-read my email and realised the autocorrect had struck. It said: *I'm sorry but I'm carrying acid in my backpack and the schoolwork just can't fit anymore.* Poor Mr Brown! I often wondered if he thought I was making up the problems we were having. I'm sure that email gave him food for thought.

CHAPTER 10

More spirit-town goodness

It was our first time in Vietnam. As soon as we landed at Danang Airport, about 30 minutes from Hội An, we knew we were somewhere special.

Botanic Gardens Villas had arranged a driver to pick us up, and Emmie was again thrilled to spot our name on a placard as we walked out into the arrivals terminal. We left the airport and set off in the dark, over the Han River and its colourful, flashing, dragon-shaped bridges. We felt happy and at peace straight away. Hội An was our second spirit town. It had been a good decision to come here.

Our room cost $22 a night and included breakfast. There were three swimming pools scattered across the Botanic Gardens properties, which stretched up a small street about a ten-minute bike ride from town and a bit longer from the beach. The street was bumpy and potholed, and at night we'd spot frogs jumping along the road as locals glided past on pushbikes and motorbikes. Families lived here in their two- and three-storey concrete-and-tiled homes, and in the mornings many would open their doors to sell steaming bowls of pho to workers on their way out for the day. Everyone rode bikes, and our guesthouse kindly gave us a pushbike with padding on the back for Emmie to sit on.

'Hello! Welcome!' Kylie and her boys yelled as they cycled into the guesthouse courtyard the next morning. I kind of recognised her from school, but it had been a while. She was tiny and bright with brown hair, sparkling eyes and a huge smile. She seemed so confident, and we loved her straight away. Her boys were lovely, too, and Emmie was happy to have two instant friends. We jumped on our bike—Emmie straddling the little seat behind me—and followed Kylie and the boys on a cycling tour around town as she pointed out everything we needed to know from the luxury of her electric bike, no pedalling required.

'Oh my gosh, you're hilarious,' I screamed as she sailed past us with her legs in the air, while I pedalled hard to keep up.

The international school I'd enrolled Emmie in, Green Shoots, was only a kilometre or so from our guesthouse, an Aussie cafe called Dingo Deli was just down the road, and we were only minutes from all the fresh local food we could eat.

That afternoon, we cycled down to the ancient town, with Emmie wearing a bright green *Monsters Inc.* helmet that Kylie had given her, arms wrapped tight around me. We zoomed through the roaring traffic, dodging motorbikes and taking off fast from the traffic lights, singing and laughing in the sunshine.

We wandered the old town, stopped for pho and the Hội An specialty, *cao lau* made with pork and noodles, dodged rickshaws and bought small bags of dried coconut to munch on. We effortlessly slipped into life in Hội An as the town and its beautiful people stole our hearts. We'd found another place that loved us back.

It just takes one person to make you feel like you belong. Kylie did that for us, welcoming us and showing us around her town, introducing us to her friends and giving us the confidence to explore on our own, tearing around the busy streets using my pedal power with Emmie sitting behind me. I made a promise that I would be that one person to as many people as I could.

The night before her first day of school, Emmie's tooth fell out, and she proudly took it to class the next day to show everyone. We walked through the gates, and she gave me a big hug and kiss before running over to her class and joining them for stretches in the garden. There were only ten kids in her Year 1 class, and they left their shoes at the door before entering the classroom, hugging or fist-bumping their teacher Miss Belinda as they went inside. Emmie gave her teacher a big hug, and I immediately fell in love with this school and turned away with happy tears in my eyes. I knew she would be looked after.

I missed her that first day. I felt like a part of me wasn't there, and I'd find myself looking for her. I thought I would love the freedom, but instead I felt lost. I missed my little shadow. When I picked her up, she had a big grin on her face and told me how she had made new friends, played games, practised 'th' words, and learned about respectful behaviours and money. She'd had a fun, easy day. Being here in Vietnam with everything falling into place was more proof that when you're on the right path, good things happen, and they happen easily.

171

This school life was so different to our schooling memories from home, of me racing off to work after getting the lunch made, leaving Coco, then Viktoria, to get Emmie to and from school. Like many working parents, I could never make it to school activities or to volunteer to help with reading or work in the canteen, and I hated missing it. I hated not being able to kiss her goodbye each morning or see her face at the end of school so I could tell how her day had been.

In Vietnam, we lived an entirely different life. Every morning we would wander from our room to breakfast, and Emmie would eat her eggs, muffins and fruit. Then, helmets on, we would climb onto the bike, wave goodbye to the guesthouse staff, and I would double Emmie to school. Her little arms would cling to me, and we'd chat and sing songs in the Hội An heat as I dodged motorbikes, taxis and potholes.

Sometimes our friends Karina and Gemma would be riding up our street from their place, and we would all ride to school together. I'd drop Emmie off then I'd go back and grab a pho from a home just across the road from our guesthouse, parking my bike in the front yard and sitting at a small table in the concrete garage. The pho was 80 cents a bowl, and the owner would ladle me a big helping of broth over noodles and thin strips of beef as we giggled at my poor attempts at Vietnamese. I could pronouce 'xin chao' ('hello') alright, and would always get an answer. But my 'Bạn co khỏe không?' ('How are you?') would leave locals either looking confused or laughing. But I kept trying!

The owner would bring me over a rectangular red plate heaped with leafy green herbs, and we'd chop chilli with her scissors and add it to the top of my pho. I'd sit there with local families and smile and eat and just love being a part of this world. Then I'd ride to a cafe, where I would meet Kylie for a coffee and work until it was time to pick Emmie up. The day was mine.

I had time to write and started trying to make an income on the road. I still had about half of my savings in the bank, and I was getting a decent amount in rent for our home, although more than half of that went onto the mortgage. More money was always going out than coming in, and I was hoping that I could start earning a little so we could stay away for longer. I spent my time writing blog posts and articles and playing around on Instagram, which didn't earn me money but I loved it! I'd answer questions from mums and dads about travelling and chat to everyone, post my photos and share what we had been doing and how we were feeling—the good, the challenges, the highs and the mistakes. I've always loved Instagram, but it was easy to get insta-obsessed and there were times when I'd be way too into my phone. If I felt that was happening, or that I was spending too much time working, I would pull back. Emmie and I set off travelling to be together, not to have me on technology all the time.

When it was time to collect Emmie, I would jump on the bike and pedal up to the school. She would climb on the back, and we'd head for the beach, a ride around the rice paddies, or home for a swim. Occasionally, the rain would pour down and flood the streets in an instant. It was late in the year, and we were heading into rainy season. The first time it happened, I was on my way to pick Emmie up from school when massive black and grey clouds full of cracking bursts of lightning suddenly took over the sky, strong winds swept down the streets and thunder rolled above me. I hunched over the handlebars in a singlet and shorts, riding my little bike through growing puddles and dodging motorcyclists in ponchos. I was saturated in seconds and almost blinded by the pouring rain, but I pushed on, anxious to get to Emmie on time. At school, I wrung waterfalls out of my clothes while we waited undercover, laughing at how wet I was, until the storm slowed. Eventually it moved on, leaving the alleyways flooded to shin height. I pushed the bike through the deep water with Emmie on the seat with her legs up over the handlebars, and we sloshed back to our guesthouse. That afternoon, I bought us both durable long ponchos that never left our bags.

Sometimes we would wander the streets of the old town, get a dress made by a tailor or go hang at a cafe and eat, eat, eat. One of our favourite spots was Mango Mango restaurant, owned by our friends Duc and Ly. I would sit in the window and sip an Asian Invasion ginger cocktail and watch as Emmie played in the street. Vendors threw their flying bird toys into the air, and she would run to catch and twirl them, laughing and enjoying her freedom among the chaos of the tourist crowds. The coloured lanterns that hung elegantly across the streets of the ancient town would glow and reflect in the water, while tourists released their floating candles from rowboats on Thu Bon River, making wishes for happiness, luck and love.

We made friends with locals and families from all over the world through Emmie's school, and we felt peace in this easy way of living, so different to life at home. Emmie often had playdates, especially with her very best classmates Nina, Than and Mai, and I loved that her closest friends were Vietnamese.

A lot of Aussies were living in town or down at the beach, working on aid projects or running successful businesses. Tanya ran the Swim Vietnam project, and Jeannie looked after an aid project that supported families in need. Travis and a few other

Aussie ex-pat businessmen ran a Nippers session every weekend, and Emmie and I would pedal down to the beach early in the morning to join in. I helped in the surf while Emmie and the kids ran flag races and swam out and around the parents positioned past the breakers. It was a lovely connection to home.

We were in Hội An for five weeks, and then it was school holidays. Rainy season was setting in, so Emmie and I travelled to the Philippines to meet Mum, Dad and Ren. Mum and Dad had splurged and paid for us all to stay in connecting rooms at the Shangri-La, and we appreciated it so much we hardly left the resort.

While we were in Manila, we went to a local studio for a live interview with the Australian TV program *The Morning Show*. I'd had a story published in the Huffington Post about how it was cheaper for us to travel in Asia than to live in Sydney, and *The Morning Show* had contacted me and asked to chat about it. I was so nervous that I'd had to get Ren to bring me my panic-attack pills from home, and I took some before we went on. Emmie wasn't a bit worried, and was ready for her big hello. 'Hi Larry, Hi Kylie,' she practised in preparation for her big moment. But there was a delay on the line, so as she spoke, so did they, and she was put off—we both were. Unfortunately, the connection was so bad that the interview ended pretty quickly. It was a bit of an anticlimax, but I didn't mind. I was so nervous that I was just glad it was over. Lots of people messaged me on Instagram to say they'd seen it, and they said it was fine, so I felt a little better.

Mum, Dad and Ren sucked up as much time with Emmie as they could, spending every minute together. We had a great family week in Manila, and when they left for Sydney, Emmie and I set off to explore the islands of the Palawan province.

In Coron, we swam at waterfalls and took boat trips around jungle-covered karst mountains jutting out of the ocean, swam into sunken volcanoes, snorkelled over shipwrecks and ate picnics on white-sand beaches. We met a local family and went to church with them one morning, joining in as they held hands and joyfully sang hymns. It was so uplifting to watch and be part of, and another way to give thanks. I had tears from the love in the room, but we now felt more at home with incense, quiet hymns and soft chanting. The serenity of the temples spoke to us.

In El Nido, while paddling beneath limestone mountains with Emmie sitting on the front of a kayak, I realised that I'd lost my GoPro with all the photos from our travels on it. We searched the water, but I resigned myself to never seeing it again. I was down for a while, but then I told myself to get over it. I'd lost heaps of things while travelling, and I reminded myself that possessions aren't important. While I loved taking photos, Emmie and I always said that the best photos were taken with our eyes and put into our memories. Later that afternoon, when we returned to our guesthouse, a local man was waiting for us. He dangled my GoPro from his fingers.

'Did you lose this today?' he asked, holding it out for me.

I couldn't believe it. Emmie and I looked at each other in happiness, and I almost cried from his kindness. This young man had been working on a tour boat and heard me asking everyone if they'd seen the GoPro. Later, he had gone looking and found it on the bottom of the lagoon (surprise! The cheap flotation handle I'd bought had failed). He'd asked around for where we were staying, and when he finished work he brought it to us. We thanked him, and I asked him to wait so I could give him something. He didn't want to, but Emmie wrapped her arms around his waist so he couldn't escape, while I ran to our room and grabbed my wallet to give him a small gift. He could easily have sold the GoPro for a few hundred dollars, but he went out of his way to find us and return it instead. How lovely is kindness from strangers without the expectation of anything in return?

This was a contented time for me and Emmie. The last time we'd been in the Philippines, we'd had to leave early because of my burst eardrum. Now we had a chance to explore a little more, and it was so worth it. The beach, water and sunshine were so good for our happiness, and we were free again, enjoying the ocean, the palm trees, snorkelling, waterfall jumping and living a wild life under the blue sky.

⌣

Our travels were never geographically organised, or really any kind of organised, to be honest. We'd left Vietnam for the Philippines, and we were now heading to Cambodia, Vietnam's next-door neighbour. We zigzagged all over Asia, travelling wherever the wind took us. It didn't bother me, though, as we're not linear by nature. We go with the flow, and there are worse things than following your heart.

All the same, I love overland travel and wish we'd done more of it. We saw so much of a country that way, like communities untouched by tourism, living in traditional villages on land their families had owned for generations. We travelled with locals heading to see beloved family or setting off to find work and earn money to send home, and had small glimpses into a daily life that seemed simpler. We saw real life under the hot sun and in green fields and gritty back streets. These are the places where the real

177

world breathes. When we travelled by air, we went from one sterile airport to the next, even though we had moved to a new country with its own story, and we missed the heartbeat of the land.

We arrived in Siem Reap, plopping down into the third spirit town of our trip and delighted to be there. We found a small guesthouse that was just a short walk away from the centre of town, super cheap at US$16 a night including breakfast, with big rooms and a good-sized swimming pool that was absolutely necessary because it was boiling hot. We wandered into town and found the hawker market, getting our first fix of Khmer curry and coconut shakes. There's nowhere else in the world that makes coconut shakes like Cambodia (apart from the Bikini Toppings cafe in Melaka, Malaysia!)

The plight of the Khmer people is truly heartbreaking. I'm not an expert on international relations or Khmer history, and it's very complex, but I learned that the population was almost wiped out during the years of the Khmer Rouge. The Khmer Rouge had a plan to start the country at Year Zero and tried to eliminate anyone who could possibly question them. Anyone who was intelligent, free-thinking or talented like artists, doctors, architects, government workers or people who had held positions within companies was executed. No one was safe. You could be turned in by a neighbour who held a grudge and be murdered or spend years in a torturous prison camp. The world turned away; no one seemed to care.

When the war was over, the country had been decimated. A shocking two-thirds of the population had been murdered or died during the Khmer Rouge's reign, and much of the country's buildings and infrastructure had been destroyed. Its roads and transport networks didn't work, its industry had ceased, and its remaining people were exhausted, displaced and traumatised, many searching for family members. But the Khmer people kept pushing on, and slowly they began rebuilding their country.

⌣

We realised early on in our travels that where we spent our money was one of the most important decisions we could make. If we only stayed, ate and explored with big businesses, tours or government-owned companies, it would be unlikely that much of our money would get to the local people. As much as possible, we used local drivers, ate at family-owned cafes and restaurants, and stayed at local guesthouses. I kept searching for more ways that we could help the Khmer people. Sometimes we got it wrong, but sometimes we got it right, and we learned a lot about ethical travel and doing things that actually help families and communities.

Many families in Cambodia live in poverty, and often children work the streets to earn money. It has one of the highest rates of child trafficking and abuse in the world, and one of the highest infant mortality rates in South East Asia—a shocking one in every 29 children will die before their fifth birthday due to poverty and a lack of access to health care. I wanted to help as much as I could, and when I found out that I could donate blood at the Angkor Hospital for Children, I was onto it.

Blood supplies are generally quite low in Cambodia, as the Khmer people are reluctant to donate blood, worrying it will affect their health and make them weak. Donating blood was one of the best ways I found to give back to this beautiful community and especially to help children who were sick with dengue fever or other illnesses.

With Patsy, a young Filipino backpacker we'd met, we set off from our guesthouse for the hospital one morning and waited at the hospital gate. The security guard let us in and gave us a visitor's pass each. Inside the gate, in the open air and the heat of the day, mums and dads sat on metal seats with their children, some attached to IV lines and lying on benches, waiting to be seen by doctors. Children lay in their mother's arms or on mats on the ground, fanned by parents with pieces of cardboard. Families had bags of food with them, and there were public cooking areas for them to prepare meals. It was heartbreaking.

'Mummy, I feel sad for the children,' Emmie whispered. 'What's wrong with them?'

'I'm not sure, Emmie,' I answered, shocked and wondering what else we could do to help. 'I guess they're sick, but at least they're here at the hospital where they can get help. And giving blood will help kids that need it, so at least we are doing something for them.'

We went up a set of stairs to a modern waiting area, where we were welcomed by the technician, a young man named Nit Nin.

'Are you scared, Mum?' Emmie asked. 'They are going to take all your blood, and what will you do then?'

'It's okay, Emmie. Our bodies are so awesome, they can make more blood. There's no reason not to share.'

'Really?'

'Really.'

'Oh, then that's okay, Mum. I'm so glad you can share your blood.'

Nit Nin gave Patsy and me some forms to complete and began preparing the room, with his new shadow Emmie trailing behind.

'Excuse me, Nit Nin, but how much blood will you take from my mum? Where does it go? Does it hurt? How big is the needle?'

'Emmie, come and sit down and let Nit Nin do his job! This is a serious business, missy.' I called her over, but Nit Nin was kind and patient, and he explained what he was doing while Emmie listened closely. I sat at his desk while he took a small vial of blood from each of us and tested our haemoglobin count.

It's been drilled into me ever since I first started travelling years ago to watch everything when getting medical treatment, to make sure every needle is new and every piece of equipment is sterile. Without me asking, Nit Nin showed us the new packets of gloves and alcohol swabs and needles as he prepared the equipment.

Patsy and I got the thumbs up from our first test and moved into the donation room, where we reclined on comfy beds. With a tiny prick, the needle was in my vein first go. Emmie danced around taking selfies, relieved that it was so simple and I wasn't in pain. My blood flowed and I felt so good about it, and soon it was over. It felt like the most precious gift I could give and hopefully I'd contributed to saving a child's life. After a little rest, Patsy and I were given biscuits and a drink (and Nit Nin kindly gave our support crew—Emmie—some, too), and we left with happiness in our hearts.

We walked through the gates and returned with fruit for the families waiting inside, and then we wandered down to our favourite little cafe on the river, Sister Srey, owned by two lovely Aussie sisters who had set off to travel years ago and stayed here, becoming part of the community and training locals in hospitality.

We sat at the open windows and watched the parade of locals, tourists and backpackers strolling by the river, brightly dressed ladies wheeling old metal ice-cream carts, workers on the riverbank preparing for the upcoming water festival, and smiling tuk tuk drivers scanning the footpath as they slowly motored past on the hunt for fares. I don't know what it was about Cambodia, but it got right into my heart, under my skin. I felt connected, with a strong love and admiration for this country and its people. I think it partly came from the kindness and optimism of the resilient Khmer and the backdrop of its tragic history.

Each day, Emmie and I strolled Siem Reap's chaotic streets in the heat, enjoying the dusty rawness and energy of the town, stopping for a foot massage and a coconut shake, so happy we could take it slow and enjoy our time there for as long as we liked. One night at dinner at the Try Me cafe across the road from our guesthouse, we met an ex-pat couple who were living in Siem Reap with their two kids. Mel and Phil ran a health and nutrition program in the South Sudan war zone for many years, and Mel was now working at an international school in Siem Reap while Phil home-schooled their two boys. We met them for putt-putt golf (a free beer for every hole-in-one!), visited their home and watched the boat races on the river together, delighted to have met such inspiring people whose lifestyle choices validated our own. I was realising the only limitations I had were the ones I put on myself.

There was so much to see and do in this beautiful town. We travelled to the gorgeous Tonlé Sap and took a boat up to the stilt-house villages built over the water. A local mum rowed us around the lake on a bamboo raft, her swaddled son beside her as we glided through narrow gaps in the long reeds, the dappled sunlight making patterns on the lake's surface. Children jumped from their stilt houses, backflipping and diving into the water as we cheered and clapped.

We watched the sun set over the lake, and on the way back our boat driver misjudged the distance between his boat and another, tearing a hole it, so we tipped him a little extra for the repairs, even though I was pretty sure he'd had a few too many beers at sunset and was drunk-boating.

In Siem Reap, we enjoyed the rewards of slow travel, wandering around as we wanted and spending time exploring the town. After a lazy morning, we set out on an afternoon walk, stopping at a Buddhist temple, Wat Preah Ang Chorm, where we could hear chanting and singing coming from groups of monks and worshippers. We said prayers, burned incense, were blessed by the monks, and sat and soaked it all in, listening to the sounds of the bamboo xylophones and feeling calm and happy. Suddenly I felt so emotional and tears came from nowhere. They were happy tears, tears of joy. I looked over at Emmie and she was the same, just glowing with happiness.

'Mummy, I feel harmony,' she said. The timing was perfect, the restful morning brought us to where we needed to be at the right minute. 'I want to feel like this all the time, Mum,' Emmie said as we wandered over to the lotus stalls to buy some offerings for the temple.

'It's beautiful, isn't it, Emmie?' I gave her a little hug. Oh, we were so content.

We spent days at Angkor exploring the ancient city, hiring a young bloke and his tuk tuk to take us around early in the morning before the heat of the day and the busloads of tourists arrived. We stopped at awe-inspiring ancient temples such as Ta Prohm, slowly being reclaimed by the jungle, and 12th-century Bayon, with its 216 gigantic carved smiling faces. We drove out to the Phnom Kulen waterfall, where novice monks swam beside us in their orange robes, and a guide took us up the 1000 Lingas river, showing us 11th-century carvings in tribute to the god Shiva, who was said to have blessed the water flowing from the mountain to Siem Reap. We arranged to see the sunrise at Angkor Wat, and we stood in the darkness waiting for the golden glow to rise over this majestic temple. It was beautiful, spiritual, even with hundreds of people jostling for space.

As we wandered towards the temple, I dropped my lens cap and as I bent down to pick it up, I felt my cheap backpacker pants tear and a soft breeze where there shouldn't be one. I swore quietly. 'Emmie, I've split my pants,' I whispered to her in horror and desperation. 'Can you see my bum?'

Of course, she thought it was hilarious. 'Oh Mum, let me see,' she said, making a big deal of inspecting me. 'Nope, it looks okay. If you keep your bag over it, you'll be alright.'

Excited stall holders were almost throwing their wares at me with the potential of a sale, but I held firm. If I wore my daypack low, tucked the torn material between my legs and moved quickly, I could make it through the temple undercover. Apart from Emmie sticking her hand in and widening the hole whenever she could, I think I slipped under the radar.

We walked up to sacred Angkor Wat to explore this delicate, beautiful heart of Cambodia. Inside in the coolness of the sandstone walls, under carvings of Aspara dancers, Emmie knelt in front of a monk for a blessing, hands clasped in prayer, as holy water was flicked on her head. I can't describe the feelings and emotions that came with knowing we were living our lives the best way we possibly could. Those special moments were everything.

Afterwards, we sat at one of the makeshift cafes in front of the temple. While Emmie played in the dirt with local kids, I had a coconut shake and enjoyed our slow pace of life and the majesty of Angkor Wat. We were right where we were meant to be.

⌣

Travelling with Emmie was mostly pretty easy. We had the same challenges that we would have had at home—mealtimes, bedtimes, manners and schoolwork—but we experienced them in amazing locations all over Asia, which I think made everything easier to handle. Of course, I had grumpy days as well. I was probably pretty hard on Emmie at times. Maybe my expectations were too high—I didn't have any other six- or seven-year-olds to compare her to. She was a good kid, but like all kids, she could be naughty, resistant and just a real pain (I could be, too). And she never packed, no matter how much I asked her. That drove me crazy, because I was always doing all the packing. But that was it, really. All things considered, she was a pretty cool kid.

'Emmie, we're leaving, hon. Make sure your daypack is ready,' I'd say as I shoved our gear into our one big pack and organised my daypack and shoulder bag.

'Sure, Mama,' she would say, and then half an hour later I'd see nothing had been done at all. Or the bag was full of rocks and random pieces of paper, and the actual stuff that needed to go in wouldn't fit. Sometimes, she seemed to delight in getting me going. This parenting thing is not easy, especially when you're solo, on the road and doing everything. Sometimes it was really hard. Emmie could be difficult and I could be short-tempered, especially when I was tired or trying to get her to do her schoolwork.

I was so invested in her happiness that any time she had a bad mood, a complaint or was rude, it felt like a personal attack. I found it so upsetting that I would then get sad and anxious. If Emmie wanted me to do something for her, even if she was capable, I would just do it because I felt guilty *all the time*, as most mums seem to. Making a decision to stop taking everything so personally really helped me be less sensitive, and once I realised that Emmie truly was happy just being with me, I stopped worrying about her not having friends her own age next to her all the time.

⌣

It was time to leave Siem Reap. We set off to teach English at a school in Battambang, a city in Cambodia's north-west with beautiful French colonial architecture and the original Phare Ponleu Selpak Circus.

'Hmm … how to get to Battambang, Emmie? What should we do?'

We were trying to find the best way to get there—private car, bus, or … boat! Wow, how lucky that we were here in the right season to get a small boat along the Tonlé Sap River to Battambang. I asked our guesthouse about it and, within minutes, we were booked on the following day's trip.

I was feeling uneasy about the English teaching in Battambang. It had been recommended by a lot of people in a world schooling Facebook group I was part of, but when I thought about it, it didn't seem right. I wanted to give back to the Khmer people, and back then I'd thought that helping to teach English would be another way I could contribute. Now that we'd been travelling for a while, I wasn't so sure. I wanted to cancel, but I'd already arranged it with the school principal and I didn't want to let him down. We continued on to Battambang with a feeling in my gut that we were doing the wrong thing.

There was no unease on the boat, though. This boat trip was another incredible adventure on our journey. Early in the morning, a tuk tuk collected us from our guesthouse and dropped us on the outskirts of town, where we waited with a bunch of tourists until a small, crowded minibus arrived. Somehow, we all folded ourselves in. I have never seen so many people in a van; it was like one of those clown cars, except that there really were 30 people inside the van.

'Mummy, is it normal in Cambodia to be so squashed in like this, do you think?' asked Emmie.

'Ha, probably,' I said as a bloke shoved a long selfie stick in front of us to take a photo of the crowd and we pulled faces for the camera.

The van lumbered off and soon we arrived at the port, where we grabbed our packs and bolted down the old wooden jetty towards the boat so we could get the pick of the spots. As the crew tied our packs to the flat roof of the boat, we climbed aboard and claimed our seats. Once the bags and people were all loaded, we realised that we could climb up to the roof.

'Mum, come on, let's go to the top,' said Emmie.

We went to the front of the little boat and climbed up a small ladder onto the roof to check it out as we set off downriver. It was a spectacular view over the massive blue lake, and we picked our way over the people already up there, found a little space and settled down for the ride.

There are some experiences I find hard to describe because they are pure, full of overwhelming joy and happiness, and just stick in my heart. They're a feeling, a memory I struggle to put into words. This was one of them. I sat on the roof of this small boat on the Tonlé Sap River in Cambodia with my little girl in my arms, leaning up against backpacks as the boat gently nosed a path through long grass, twisted brown trees with branches that reached out to scratch us, and long reeds that whipped against our legs. We passed villages built on stilts over the water, and kids playing, poking around in canoes and jumping from their wooden huts straight into the flowing river. Groups of happy children in loose clothes smiled and waved to us from the shore, and fishermen threw nets buoyed by empty plastic bottles into the river, waiting in the sunshine in their wooden canoes to haul them back in. Emmie fell asleep, and as I lay our sarong over her to protect her from the sun, I thanked the universe for bringing me right here. The most precious moments are when we are together, out in the world, holding hands and just being close. There's a peacefulness, a connection. It's just us and the world. The beautiful, breathtaking world.

After seven hours of rocking, swaying and enjoying the peace on the rooftop with a bunch of chilled strangers, we arrived in Battambang as the sun set. We clambered off, stiff-legged, tired and content, and everyone scattered. I grabbed a tuk tuk driver, who helped us carry our pack up the bank, and together we figured out where we were going, hunched over my phone in the darkness. The driver didn't the know the address I showed him, but he recognised the school principal's name and knew where to take us.

We were staying with the principal and his family in his rather large house near the school. It was tiled and cool, and we dropped our bags off and followed the principal down to the dirt path to the school in the moonlight. It had four wooden classrooms, an office with a couple of old computers, and a hut with some cooking utensils. We joined him and his wife for dinner and sat outdoors around a small table with food cooked on an open fire. Emmie tucked into the boiled rice, and I tried the river frog they offered. I couldn't bring myself to eat it all, but I understood how very generous they were in sharing their food with us.

The next morning, as we were about to start the volunteer teaching work, Emmie came to me, looking upset. 'I'm scared, Mummy,' she said, putting her little arms around my neck and resting her head on my shoulder.

'Oh, Emmie, what are you worried about?' I asked. I knew something was up.

'Of you being a good teacher.'

I understood. 'You're worried I'll get better at it and find ways to force you to do your work, is that it?' I asked.

'Yes.' She nodded, in tears.

'Oh well, don't worry. I'll be as hopeless as always,' I told her.

'Yay!' she said with a big smile.

I constantly waver between admiration and eye-rolling with this one.

The first day of teaching wasn't very nice. The principal had gone away early in the morning, and had told me to just rock up with Emmie and help at the school. I wasn't even sure if the teachers knew we were coming, but it was soon very clear that they didn't want us there. We had to make our own way into the classroom, and I assumed that they would be welcoming, but the first teacher didn't even let us in the room. He shut the door as he saw us coming and didn't answer my knocks.

I was in tears, but I understood where he was coming from. It must be just so disruptive to have Western tourists strolling into class, thinking they are being helpful but just being a nuisance. It was condescending to these qualified teachers. What could I offer? I wasn't a teacher, I was just a blow-in who thought I was helping. And I didn't have any idea how to teach English! I wanted to leave, but at the same time we had made a commitment, so we stayed and did a few small sessions with the kids in another class.

We weren't even adding value, apart from helping to correct pronunciation. I felt awful.

I soon realised that the best way to help a school is to buy the kids notebooks, pens, atlases, geometry and protractor sets—basically anything they can use to help their learning—or to support reputable organisations that exist to improve children's education. Visiting schools, visiting orphanages, volunteering at schools: none of it helps the children. It's just distracting for them and, in some cases, supporting evil industries where children are taken from their parents so organisations can earn money through donations from tourists.

After a few days, we left the principal's home and moved into a small guesthouse in town. We were used to having our own space, and it was nice to wander around whenever we wanted. Plus, I could also go into the school less if we stayed in town. There was a coffee shop with big comfy lounges, and we hung out there most mornings—Emmie could even get her favourite breakfast, bacon and eggs. We bumped into a family of missionaries we'd seen in a bookshop in Siem Reap, made friends with a couple of American girls who were working there as part of their religious service and met up with the principal's teenage daughters for meals.

Each morning, we woke early to give alms to the monks as they glided around town in their orange robes holding woven baskets. They moved so fast that sometimes we would have to run down the street to get in front of them. We would take our shoes off, bow our heads and carefully place our money in the monks' bowl, making sure to not touch them. It was beautiful, but when we were running and trying to figure out what street they would go to next, it would make me laugh at the absurdity of us on our morning monk missions.

In the evenings, we'd walk along the riverfront as locals exercised, danced and did aerobics in groups to 1980s pop music blasting from little cassette radios, and we joined in a few times. It was so much fun, and Emmie got a good laugh out of it as we tried to keep up with the choreography.

One night, we noticed a bloke on a bike with a rider on the back waving to us. It was Greg and Simone from the bus in Malaysia! 'Evie! Evie!' they yelled. It was so bizarre to see them again—out of all the people we'd met so far—and we said hello and had a chat. I just hoped they would find their way around the country okay. If anyone was going to get into trouble, I felt it would be inappropriate Greg. I wonder where they ended up.

We'd heard a lot about Battambang's bamboo train, and we caught a tuk tuk out to the station to explore. These trains started operating in the 1980s and were built by survivors of the Khmer Rouge using the materials they could find—bamboo, old motors from bikes and boats, and wheels taken from old and destroyed cars. During the war, roads had been heavily damaged, and afterwards workable cars and bikes were scarce and landmines littered the countryside. The little bamboo trains were used to transport people, crops and livestock along the remaining tracks.

We paid US$5 and jumped aboard a bamboo platform covered with a small blanket. The driver sat at the back of the platform and used a stick attached to a rubber band in the old motor to speed up and slow the car. Off we went, so fast it was kind of terrifying, especially with all the bumps and wiggles along the tracks, as we flew past fields and over bridges. Soon enough, there was someone coming towards us. Being a single track, there's no passing, so we stopped and got off our bamboo platform. Our driver lifted it off its wheels and popped it on the grass on the side of the tracks.

191

He then took the wheels off the track, and the other car passed. Our car was reassembled and then off we went again. Brilliant.

We were having a great time, but our experience at the school had been so deflating, I just wanted to move on. We decided to finish our time early and bought the children new writing books and pens to say thank you for having us. It was a big learning experience, and I was sad that I went against my gut, but in a way I'm also glad we did because I often share this mistake and hope others won't make it, too.

The best thing we did in Battambang was to visit the Phare Ponleu Selpak Circus. The staff told us that the circus had started at a refugee camp on the Thai–Cambodian border in 1986. A French humanitarian worker used art as a way to help the thousands of orphaned children to try to cope with the trauma they'd experienced. After returning to Battambang in 1992, a group of young men came together to continue the program using art as therapy. It grew from one drawing class to a school that helps Cambodian children and families with education, support and social services through art, music and performance.

It's crazy to think that this was all happening just over 30 years ago, and inspiring to see what can be achieved by selfless people working together to help others. We sat in the big top and watched an emotional performance by Khmer dancers who had trained and learned here, their lives so very different from ours.

It was time to go, so we set off for Phnom Penh. Christmas was fast approaching, and I'd been deliberating about what to do. I was worried about our budget and having to book accommodation at Christmas prices. We wanted to stop, chill and not move around. A house-sit in Wuxi, China—just two hours north of Shanghai by train—came up on TrustedHousesitters (a house-sitting site we'd joined before leaving Australia), and we applied and got it, quite possibly because we were the only applicants. We had to go to Phnom Penh to apply for another China visa, so we set off along the bumpy road out of Battambang.

~

After eight hours on an ancient bus that had groaned and rattled along potholed roads beside green fields, elegant faded villages and a sun that lowered behind distant Phnom Oudong, the old Khmer capital, we arrived in Phnom Penh. As usual, Emmie had stretched out across me, put her head down and slept the whole way. I'd listened to music, watched passengers pull fried insects dripping with oil from plastic bags for snacking, and tried to absorb the beautiful scenery as it flashed past—the rice paddies almost fluorescent under the setting sun, the wide, open sky and the tiny children playing in the dirt in front of rickety wooden shacks. There was so much beauty in basic life in Cambodia.

Stretching and dragging our pack behind us, we climbed from the bus into a crowd of tuk tuk drivers waiting for their tourist fare. I love Khmer tuk tuks: they're like miniature chariots with a motorbike in front and two seats facing each other in the back with lots of space and curtains to shield you from the noise and chaos outside. The Khmer have style, that's for sure.

We watched two German ladies with amusement as they vigorously tried to bargain down a ride. Failing, they turned in disgust and stomped off into the night, dragging their wheelie bags behind them. That used to be me, the budget backpacker. Now, I handed our pack to the first driver who approached us and agreed to a $4 fare across the city to our guesthouse.

We jumped into the tuk tuk, and the driver perched our pack behind him as we rode towards our guesthouse, dodging hundreds of motorbikes along wide, decrepit streets lined with crumbling facades, ornate gates and pretty painted walls. Men and women rode bicycles weighed down with colourful rice cakes for sale, food carts lined the streets and I got the sense, as I had since we arrived in Cambodia, that everyone was working hard to make a better life for their family and community.

'Hold your bags tight,' the driver told us as we set off into the darkness. 'It is not safe here.'

Phnom Penh gave me bad juju, but I couldn't put my finger on why. It lacked the warmth of Siem Reap and the authenticity of Battambang. I felt like there was a dangerous underbelly, a dark energy bubbling below the surface. It's not surprising. The city was devastated during the years of the Khmer Rouge, at first overpopulated with domestic refugees and then evacuated, looted and left to fall apart. The S21 prison was here, and the Killing Fields were not far away. Rebuilding began in the 1980s, and while beautiful French colonial architecture and decorative facades of Khmer temples gave glimpses of majesty, it is mostly a cacophony of loose-limbed shop fronts, overhanging wires, noisy, chaotic traffic and the struggle of poverty. Although the people were friendly, my senses told me to lay low. I just didn't have the vibe here, and I trusted my vibe.

On our first day in town, I gathered all the information we needed for our China visa application, booking flights and hotels and printing it all out. It was pretty stressful booking and paying for flights and accommodation before I knew if the visa would be approved, but that's how it had to be done. We anxiously presented it to the embassy, and they told us to come back with more details.

'Mum, you did it wrong,' Emmie said as we left, always supportive.

Our next attempt was accepted, and we had around a week to wait before we could pick up our passports, hopefully with the visas in them.

Most visitors to Phnom Penh make a beeline for the Killing Fields and Tuol Sleng Genocide Museum, on the site of the S21 prison, to learn more about the Khmer Rouge and pay their respects to the millions of families, scholars, farmers and artists who were murdered under Pol Pot's brutal regime. I would have loved to visit, but I couldn't with Emmie; she was too young. We instead spent our days drinking coffee and coconut shakes, wandering the streets and eating roadside chicken, lazing in bed and swimming in our guesthouse's rooftop pool.

Six days later, our visas were ready. We picked up our passports from the Chinese embassy and travelled south to the beach, shunning the bus for a private car. For $50, we sat in comfort as we motored past villages and temples, houses with ornate colourful gates and locals working in green fields. We passed a majestic elephant walking down the highway into Sihanoukville, its mahout on her back. It was a strange and curious sight, and I felt for this elephant walking on the concrete road in the heat of the day. I wish I had stopped, but what could I have done?

From Sihanoukville, we caught a boat over to Lazy Beach on Koh Rong Samloem and stayed in a little hut on the edge of the jungle. A slash of white sand was all that separated us from the water, and the beach reminded me of home.

We'd planned to stay here for only a few days, but then we met the Kinnairds, a beautiful family of five from Jersey in the Channel Islands. We immediately clicked. They'd been travelling for a year and were nearing the end of their adventures, and I felt lucky to meet them. Being able to stop and spend time with great people was so important—for Emmie's wellbeing and interaction with kids and for me to relax. I learned a lot from Harriet's gentle manner with her three children. I was starting to get frustrated with Emmie, and Harriet reminded me through her actions to be kinder—and I think the evening wines helped a lot, too.

We spent our days relaxing and playing in the sand and the water—reading, building sandcastles, having backgammon challenges, swimming, pier jumping, chilling on comfy lounges and hammocks, and eating all day. It was heaven.

On our way back to our cabin one night, Emmie and I noticed that the water was sparkling every time little waves curled onto the sand. It was phosphorescence! We'd tried to see it snorkelling one night in Koh Lipe, but it had been pretty lacklustre. The golden twinkles in the water in front of us now looked so magical, we ran to our hut, put our cossies on and jumped in. We stayed close to one another in the shallows, and every time we moved, we left trails of sparkles.

'Watch this, Mum,' Emmie whispered in awe as she danced her fingertips through the ocean, creating a swirl of glitter behind her. We were swimming through starlight.

⌣

I'm certain the Kinnairds were put in our way by the universe to teach us. They also rescued us when I lost all my bank cards on the way back to Phnom Penh. I messaged them, and they booked us a room in the guesthouse they were at and loaned us money to tide me over while I sorted out my cards.

I knew that we had overstayed our visa, and we should have left the country five days earlier, but we had been having too much fun with the Kinnairds at Lazy Beach to leave, and then we had the card issue. And so, after a week of overstaying, we entered the Phnom Penh International Airport with more than a little trepidation. After checking in, we approached the 'overstay visa' desk with huge smiles, ready to pay a fine, but hoping to charm our way out of it.

'Work it, Emmie. We can do this,' I said, fairly certain that we couldn't. I tried to negotiate using my smiles, my questionable grasp of very basic Khmer and Emmie's cuteness—but failed miserably.

Overstay Cambodia visa. Pay US$200.

Oh well. It was worth it.

CHAPTER 11

A year, already

We were both looking forward to being back in China. We missed the people and the energy and the chaos, and of course the *xiao long bao*. We flew to Shanghai from stinking hot Cambodia into a coldness I had totally underestimated after being in the heat of Asia for most of the past eleven months. You would think I would have checked the weather before flying out, wouldn't you? Well, I did. Kind of.

I knew it would be cold, but I just didn't give it too much thought. I intended to grab us pants and jackets while we waited for our connection at Suvarnabhumi Airport in Bangkok. There are heaps of shops there, and I was sure we could buy some clothes and arrive warm and ready for the weather. Of course, when we landed in Bangkok, we were at Don Muang Airport instead, a small budget airline transit terminal, which meant a McDonald's, a Starbucks and nothing else. It wasn't ideal, but I reckoned we could work it out when we got to Shanghai … in our summer clothes. At least I got to have a grande mocha and Emmie some nuggets while we waited for our connection.

We arrived in Shanghai at 6.00 am and found our way around the train network to Disneyland, with the help of a few kind locals. We could have taken a taxi, but my last taxi experience in Beijing had made me a little reluctant, and we had time and it saved us $40. We love the train, and, as usual, the Chinese people helped us with our bags, told us what stations to change at and directed us to the platforms. Easy! We were too early to check in at the Disneyland Toy Story Hotel, so we layered up and went to the shopping outlet just down the road, hoping to find some warm clothes. It was so cold that we were shivering as we ran from shop to shop, and Emmie was obsessed with seeing her breath cloud into white smoke. We found Emmie a jacket and boots, spending triple the money we'd just saved on the taxi. There was nothing for me, though. It was a designer outlet, and even at a discount, adult clothes were still too expensive. Had I known just how cold it would get, I probably would have paid the money … or maybe not.

The next day, we layered everything we had in our backpacks onto our bodies. Every shirt, every long-sleeved top, shorts and pants, our rain jackets and our socks—everything went on. Our legs were freezing, but at least Emmie had her new boots and a puffer jacket, and she felt warm enough. I was so cold! It was 2 degrees, and summer outfits on top of one another couldn't fix that. Sadly, I realised that my very Australian 'she'll be right, mate' attitude may not always be the best one. Certainly not this time, anyway.

Who gets around in 2-degree weather in summer tights, a few layers of thin shirts and a jumper? Well, me. But I don't recommend it. We moved fast and tried to keep some level of warmth in our bodies. It was so chilly, but there are much worse places to be freezing than Shanghai Disneyland! We warmed up in the Star Wars Launch Bay, went on all the rides over and over again, especially Emmie's favourites, TRON and Camp Discovery, and watched the parades and the fireworks.

Three days later, we were up at 5.00 am to catch a train to Wuxi, as the people we were house-sitting for were flying to the United States that day and had been pretty strict on when we needed to arrive. It was only two hours from Shanghai, so we took the 6.00 am train and then a taxi from the station, arriving at their apartment right on time. We buzzed them and they let us up, looking anxious and frustrated as they answered the door.

'We're not ready yet,' they said. 'Could you come back in two hours?'

I was a bit put out, given that we'd arrived early at their request, and were in a strange city in the middle of nowhere, but we managed to hail another taxi and directed it to a neighbouring town, where we sat in a cafe and waited until we could go back.

House-sitting in Wuxi was one of the most random things we ever did. Emmie was thrilled to be back in China, and we both appreciated having a bit of home life for a month. We were staying in a small two-bedroom apartment and looking after a sweet old dog. For the first two days, we slept and read and were just happy to do nothing (except walk Honey and pick up her poo) in our own space for a bit.

Once we started exploring, we found that Wuxi was pretty cool. While quite industrial, it was a beautiful city with an ancient town and a canal network that lit up at night with thousands of lanterns and fairy lights strung between buildings and across beautiful arched stone bridges, especially the famous Qingming Bridge that dates back to the Ming Dynasty. There were old temples and friendly locals, and it was a gorgeous city in the evening. We visited Nanchang Temple and gave offerings to the giant golden Buddha, we took boat rides along the canal and walked across bridges and along little passageways, stopping for street food and for Emmie to play on the old fairground rides that were scattered beside the path. She got an extra-long ride sitting inside half a watermelon, as the friendly owner of the ride wanted to talk about Australia with me.

We spent a day at Xihui Park, exploring temples, pagodas, archways and ancient manicured gardens, and took the chairlift to the top of Mount Hui, walking back down again and stumbling across a group of buskers with their own amps and microphones playing just outside a temple. They wanted Emmie to sing a song, but she declined. After my Filipino karaoke experience, I would have said yes, had I been asked.

Wuxi often suffers from high pollution, so our hosts had left us masks to wear when we were out and about. Elastic loops slipped over our ears, and the mask covered our mouths and noses. We wore them a few times, but they were so difficult to get used to, and no one else was wearing them, so after a while we didn't bother.

I felt like we had everything we would need for the next four weeks, especially when we discovered a Din Tai Fung on the top floor of a fancy Chinese mall. Emmie was ecstatic to have her *xiao long bao* again, especially as she was treated like a princess and given dough to play with, and staff made her cute little creatures from it. Wuxi remains her favourite Din Tai Fung of all.

'*Ni hao*,' Emmie would announce as she arrived into the restaurant, and the staff would swarm over her. She adored being the centre of attention.

One day, we were finishing our dumplings when a young girl approached our table.

'Hello. My name is Jo. My mum and aunty would like to take you to the ancient town,' she said softly, pointing over to her family, who waved at us with big smiles on their faces. It was so kind of them, and we jumped into their car out to the Huishan Ancient Town. Jo's mum and aunt showed us ancient buildings and bought us traditional sugar lollies shaped like koi before stopping at an acupuncturist where they had an appointment.

'It is very good,' Jo told me. 'He is very old and the best.'

I decided that I would have acupuncture, too, and we arranged to return in an hour. I've had a sore knee for years after having a reconstruction when I was younger and losing most of my cartilage. I'd had acupuncture before, and it had always been good for me, so I was keen to try it at the source. When we returned, the elderly man gestured for me to sit, and the first thing he did was feel my pulse, then speak to his assistant.

'You eat too much,' his assistant translated. 'And you have liver and spleen problems.'

I laughed. 'Oh, thanks so much, but what about my knee?'

For the next twenty minutes, I had acupuncture on my back and in my knee, but this doctor was not as delicate a touch as those I'd seen at home. Knee finished, he asked if he could put the needle into my top lip to help with my liver.

'Sure, no problem,' I agreed, and he thrust the needle straight in. Oh. My. God. The pain was so intense that I felt sick and dizzy, and Emmie screamed as I went white and wobbly.

With a grin, the old doctor quickly pulled the needle out.

'You do not have to pay for that needle,' his assistant told me.

I instantly recovered once the needle was out, so we decided to walk back into Wuxi town, or at least try to get as far as we could before we hailed a taxi. Wandering through a park, we stumbled upon a group of men sitting on a circular concrete seat, all with small wooden bird cages. Inside were songbirds that were there to hang out, as were the men. It's said that a songbird that doesn't get outside and have a chance to be with other birds will lose its voice, so daily walks and gatherings are important. It felt like a special cultural moment to me, but the men didn't seem happy to see us and quickly covered their cages ... so we wandered on across the river and back into town.

Livat was our favourite mall in Wuxi. It had a huge indoor climbing and zipline area, a massive ball pit, movie theatres, lots of toy stores and an ice-skating rink. I'm not big on Christmas, but I knew I needed to make Emmie's day special, so I was on the hunt for decorations. I managed to find a small Christmas tree and some tinsel at the mall, and we set up the tree in the living room. Making sure Santa had presents to leave under it was a little trickier, but on Christmas morning, there were decorations around the bed and presents under the tree. She woke up and spotted her presents straight away.

'Santa found me, Mummy,' she yelled. 'Merry Christmas! Santa found me in China.'

Santa did a good job.

We unwrapped our pressies while Skyping with my mum and dad, then got ready for our big Christmas Day—back at Livat Shopping Mall! While Christmas was just another day in China, there *was* a Christmas pantomime in the shopping centre and carols were playing, so that was enough for us. We watched the show and played in the ball pit, and Emmie flew along the ziplines and climbed and jumped and played in the adventure zone. Christmas dinner was *xiao long bao* and caramel Tim Tams we'd found in a Western supermarket in the basement of the shopping centre. It was such a good Christmas!

It was a fun few weeks, and we felt rested and ready to move on by the time our house-sit was up a week after the New Year began. We were going back to Hội An for a few months to soak up the goodness of our spirit town.

Our flight out of Shanghai was at 6.00 am, so we took a late-night train from Wuxi and a taxi from Shanghai train station to the airport, getting in at about 2.00 am. Luckily for us, Shanghai airport had what we call a Starbucks Hotel—a 24-hour Starbucks—so we pulled up our luggage trolley, I made a little bed for Emmie on my backpack, and she went to sleep while I settled in to drink coffee for the next few hours.

At about 4.00 am, my phone started buzzing with messages and emails. A story about Emmie and me had been published in the *Daily Mail* in Australia by journalist Sophie Haslett, who had interviewed me some time before, and it was getting a lot of attention. I wasn't really sure what was going on or how to deal with it, and we had a flight to catch, so I answered a few emails and gave the other journalists who'd contacted me permission to publish our story, and then we were on our way.

By the time we'd taken the plane back to Danang and a taxi to Hội An, the news story about us seemed to be everywhere. There were interview requests, stories published about us online and in newspapers and magazines all over the world, and videos about us using photos from our Instagram account. To have our story published so widely was something I'd never experienced before and it was so exciting, but it also made me uncomfortable because I couldn't completely control it. I also felt it was a missed opportunity—though for what, I didn't know.

We were in such a broad mix of online newspapers and magazines from Norway to New Zealand. The *Daily Mail* video had more than 10 million views and even more videos popped up. I'll always be very grateful to Sophie for being interested in us, as having a profile certainly helped us as we continued to travel, and more opportunities came our way.

While all this was happening, I also learned that people who comment online on news stories quite often don't have many nice things to say. I looked at the comments on some of the stories, and it seemed that for every supportive comment, there would be two really mean ones. Mostly it didn't bother me, but I couldn't understand why people would bother to spend their valuable time writing nasty comments about people they didn't know! The themes were always the same:

> *Probably took all the husband's money and is now living it up around the world.*
> *This single mum is on welfare and using the government's money to travel. What a joke.*
> *What happens when the kid gets sick? She will come home and use the government's health care that WE pay for.*

She is so irresponsible sleeping at airports. What an awful woman.
How dare she steal that child from her father.
I wonder where the father is, and if she knows who he is.
What a terrible mother taking the child away from all her friends
    just because she doesn't have a job and wants to run away.

And my favourite:
That photo is obviously the grandmother. Is there a photo of
    the mother?

Ha. I had a good laugh at that one.

At first, I tried to answer these comments and explain that no, our travels were self-funded and we had travel insurance that covered any medical problems, and that yes, her father had been consulted. I wanted to show these people why we were travelling and how good it was for Emmie, but I soon gave up. They didn't care about my answers; they just wanted to be hurtful.

Many, many people were so nice, though. Both women and men would spring to my defence. I think many were my Instagram friends, who were so kind to look after us and jump in. I felt like that a lot with our Instagram buddies: they looked after us, they wanted us to do well, to have a great adventure and succeed. They believed in us. It made me feel very secure and was a huge help to me. I never felt alone, and we always had incredible people from around the world cheering us on.

As we travelled, I shared when things were tough or when I needed help or if I'd made a mistake. I got such wonderful support and advice, and we had long conversations on my posts on Instagram where we learned so much about each other just chatting in the comments. And as for those nasty people?

Well, I've never counted countries, so I couldn't tell them how many countries Emmie has been to or how many flights she has been on to quantify the value of travelling together. What I could tell them is that she was loving our adventure. What we had together was not measured in the number of flights or countries we'd visited but in what I could see in her eyes—the sparkle, the laughter and the happiness of being with me and having the time of her life.

Emmie was happy being back in Vietnam with her friends. When her birthday rolled around, I ordered a big creamy Vietnamese cake decorated with elephants and a huge seven. It was covered with mountains of sweet mock cream, a Vietnamese specialty. I took the cake to school where her class sang 'Happy Birthday' and devoured it, then we all went to the Dingo Deli cafe for a play on the equipment out back. The ladies at the guesthouse gave Emmie little presents and another cake, and later I took her to a tailor in the ancient town, where she chose material and had a dress she had designed made for her. It was a sweet birthday: no pressure, no huge parties, just lots of love.

I could hardly believe it, but a year of travelling was coming up. A year already? It didn't seem possible. Where had the time gone? I wasn't ready to go home, and neither was Emmie. It wasn't time. I felt this strongly in my heart, in my head, in my bones. I became anxious when I thought about it. If we went home, I would have to get a job in the city, and everything would go back to what it was before. I wasn't ready to give up time with Emmie, to give up the space in my brain that was free of routine and commitments. We still had so much to see and do! We couldn't go back yet.

The Vietnamese New Year, Tet, was fast approaching, and preparations were in full swing. Kumquat trees sat in pots outside homes and businesses to bring good luck and good health. Daisies and peach blossoms filled every available space to attract lucky bees. The beautiful Vietnamese flag—bright red with the golden star in the middle—lined the streets and flew from every home. Emmie had celebrations at school and wore a traditional dress and sang Vietnamese songs.

Everyone greeted each other with *Chuc Mung Nam Moi!* Happy New Year! We shared the luck, buying a kumquat plant for the guesthouse and giving out traditional red packets with money inside to children and the staff.

Tet is all about family, so over the holiday locals travel home or their family travels to them. We decided that since Hội An would be quiet and the shops would be shut, it would be a good time for a mini-break. It was the anniversary of our year of travelling, so we wanted to do something meaningful and worthwhile to celebrate. Emmie was so interested in elephants after our time in Chiang Mai and we were keen to learn more about them, so we decided to visit the Elephant Valley Project (EVP) in Mondulkiri, Cambodia, after our Instagram friend Ellie recommended it. The EVP's approach to the elephants was focused on rehabilitation, not selfies with tourists, so it seemed like a perfect choice.

We flew into Phnom Penh and travelled in a minivan down to Mondulkiri, bumping along past fields and buffalo and crumbling houses in gated gardens with pink and red flowers winding their way over the metal fences. Many had handwritten signs thanking Australian and American donors for helping them rebuild their homes.

At the EVP, we met Jemma, the awesome Aussie manager, and her team of Western and local staff committed to elephant welfare. The EVP supports 2000 people in the community through employing locals and had also built a small school and medical centre for the village. Like many Khmer in this area, the villagers were animists and believed in the power of the universe and nature. They loved caring for elephants and the work done at the EVP.

We set off to spot elephants, walking down into the jungle to find them gathered at the river. We watched them bathe and forage in the thick green scrub, tearing off branches and devouring them, or holding them in their trunks and hoisting them over their shoulders to scratch their backs. We listened to their bellows and rumbles that rolled through the earth and could reach other elephants up to 32 kilometres away. We'd been given information cards about elephant health, and we learned that elephants regulate their temperature through their ears, just how delicate their backs are and how long they live, often in painful servitude, dragging logs and equipment for construction, carrying tourists or doing other debilitating work.

We helped with volunteer work on the river, moving logs and creating a little dam, and we slept in a small cabin overlooking the jungle, listening to the birds and the sounds of the night. It was blissful and so terribly sad. Sanctuaries like the EVP are in a tough position, as they want to rescue elephants without creating a market for rescuing elephants. It's a fine balance. Elephants are big business. It can cost up to US$20,000 to rescue an elephant from an owner who uses it for rides, and its ongoing care is significant because of the amount of food each elephant eats—more than 350 kilos a day.

Some of these rescued elephants had been chained and mistreated for 50 years, spending their whole lives in pain. We met Sambo, a new arrival, finally free after 40 years of walking the Phnom Penh riverside and doing tricks for tourists. She had been eating sugar and chip packets and Coca Cola and whatever tourists had fed her, and had slept chained up on a dirt patch with a few old banana leaves tossed her way each evening. She had abscesses the size of saucers in her feet—her sensitive pads had walked on hot asphalt day after day, and as the tread had worn away, huge holes had opened up. At the Elephant Valley Project, she had been given medical treatment and paired up with another elephant, who had taught her how to forage. Slowly, she had started adapting to a life of freedom, albeit with daily antiseptic and antibiotic treatments.

I asked Jemma about the elephant I had seen walking to Sihanoukville months ago, and she told me that she had collapsed and died on the side of the road not long after I saw her. The EVP had been trying to get the elephant for their sanctuary, but its owner wouldn't let her go. It was a sad end to a sad life of servitude travelling on hot bitumen up and down the length of the country.

Emmie's and my one-year travel anniversary arrived while we were at the EVP, and it was perfect. Wow, what a year. Our best year. It just didn't feel like a year had passed, and it made me so sad and anxious that it was coming to an end. Every precious second, every special minute, had flown by in a sparkling swirl of magical moments spent together, just me and Emmie. But surely it couldn't be a year? It felt like we only just left. What should we do? What *could* we do?

We should be going home.

We have to go back.

We don't want to go back.

We have to go back.

We don't want to go back.

Sigh.

We said our goodbyes to Jemma and the team at the EVP and moved into Sen Monorom, where we found a bloke with a car who would take us to see the Bousra Waterfall. We zoomed along, gazing out at the wide plains and tiny villages, the beauty of Cambodia always making us feel so at home. At the waterfall, monks were bathing and locals were relaxing and enjoying life in nature. And in this tiny corner of Cambodia, you will never guess what Emmie found.

A bloody zipline.

But not just any bloody zipline. This one went right over Bousra Waterfall, the highest waterfall in the country.

'Mum, look at this amazing zipline!' she said, doing game-show hands as she pointed it out to me. It wasn't enough for Emmie to visit the waterfall, marvel at the waterfall and appreciate how spectacular it was. Oh no. She wanted to zipline over it. I honestly believe her enjoyment of the zipline was in direct relation to how uncomfortable I was with it. The more I didn't want to do it, the more she loved it.

I can't stop Emmie from doing something just because I am too scared to do it myself, I thought. *And I can't let her do it alone. But I don't want to do it. But she really wants to, and I should let her.* I didn't know what to do, so I used the best excuse I had—money.

'Emmie, it's really expensive, so this time it's a no, okay?'

But my inner voice started up again. *I always said money wouldn't stop us doing anything. Ziplining over a waterfall in Cambodia, that's a once-in-a-lifetime experience and maybe we should ... But it's dangerous*

... and why didn't I bring some kind of camera to video us going over the waterfall. Oh well. Let's give it a shot.

My poor brain. 'Ugh, fine, okay. Let's go on the zipline,' I said.

'Mum, really? Really?' She was so excited. 'You're the best mum ever.'

'Yeah, I know,' I laughed. 'Now I'm the best mum ever going into a terrified coma.'

We headed over to the ziplining counter, where they were delighted to see us. I think we were their first customers in who knows how long, which didn't exactly fill me with confidence, but the two young Khmer blokes who looked after us were very professional and sweet and seemed to know their stuff. I signed the waiver, paid the money and off we went.

The young men put us into our harnesses and we stepped into our leg straps. OMG, they were so tight, cutting off the circulation in my thighs, and I was laughing and complaining. These harnesses were made for small people!

'I need you to loosen these, please. Do they go looser? I'm sorry, I'm stretching your equipment.'

The poor young blokes had to kneel down between my thighs and loosen the straps for me, but we were all laughing and already having fun. We waved goodbye to our driver and set off to the zipline course with our two lovely guides, driving around the top of the waterfall in a jeep and then walking up a path along the side of the falls.

The boys took it slowly, telling us about their people, the Bunong Tribe, who are animists and deeply connected to nature. They know every tree, the fruit and medicine it could provide or what its wood could do, and they believe that everything has a spirit—humans, nature and all living and non-living things—all working together in a relationship that protects the land. The forest is very special to the Bunong, and it hurts them to not have much left due to mining and logging.

The area we were in was a Spirit Forest, and because of the waterfall it was a place of spiritual power and home to the strongest spirits in the animist religion. The boys showed us tiny spirit houses built in the jungle by the villagers, with offerings left inside for the forest spirits. It was ancient and other-worldly and it gave me goosebumps. I was blown away by the simple beauty of this life and the respect for nature and all living things.

'Mummy, this is so beautiful,' Emmie said. 'I can feel the love for nature here. I am definitely an animist Buddhist.'

We stopped in the forest and said a prayer to the waterfall spirit to keep us safe on our journey. It was another one of those moments where my brain and my heart were so full of learning and love for this world. I adored Cambodia even more.

Soon, we were at the start of the zipline. It was a series of six smaller ziplines stretching from platform to platform, over trees and through gaps in the forest, with the last one, the big one, over the waterfall. I was terrified, even with the protection of the spirits.

We did a safety test and were given instructions on how to land. As usual, Emmie was off, scurrying up and leaping out like a little monkey, flying from tree to tree with her legs out and her arms behind her head, taunting me with her ease.

I was an entirely different story. I clutched, I screamed, I moaned and I procrastinated. It wasn't the height that bothered me, it was the leaping. It was easy for me to take my own leap when I was relying on me to catch me, but not when I was relying on others. After a few failed attempts at launching, I finally let go and hung in the air while the metal shrieked its way across the wire. I soared above the ground, coming into a crash landing on the wooden boards at the next tree.

'Evie, you must lift your legs,' the boys told me, laughing.

'I honestly thought I was,' I laughed back at them.

We zipped from platform to platform, with Emmie taking it easy and me continuing to freak out but pushing myself along. Soon, it was time for the big one.

We were really going to zipline across a waterfall. Was this a good idea? Well, it was too late now. I was going first, just in case it was about to break. I'd take the hit for the Dragon Team.

I sat on the edge in tears, looking out over the sheer drop and trying to get up the courage for this leap into the unknown. What was I waiting for? Why couldn't I let go? I'd already taken a leap into the unknown in real life, and it was the best thing I'd ever done. That leap was almost over now, though, and we didn't want it to end.

So why does it have to end?

I moved closer to the edge of the platform and stood there, gathering my courage. And then, all of a sudden, I just let go.

I was flying. Oh my God, it was incredible. I was so high above the ground, and I zoomed over the water and the rocks, beside the waterfall, with the screeching of the wires and the wind in my face. I felt so strong as I flew, and I felt the universe and the spirits whisper to me: *you don't have to go back.*

I landed, so full of joy and energy and the realisation that my decisions were in my hands. I was in control here—well, Emmie and I. It was up to us. I unclipped and waited for Emmie to soar over. Soon, she was on her way, absolutely delighted with the thrill of the ride and just loving her life. And why wouldn't she?

She had just ziplined over a waterfall in Cambodia. Her life was A-plus.

'Mum, that was the best time ever! I've had the best day ever! You're the best, Mum! Thank you!'

We wandered back to the zipline base, took off all our safety gear and our helmets, and gave the boys a tip. We spent the rest of the afternoon chatting with local families and monks, and relaxing by the falls. That night, we met up with the crew from the Elephant Valley Project and, after dinner, we wandered back down to our guesthouse along the dirt road, past roaming dogs and open-air classrooms filled with people of all ages learning English.

'Hey, Emmie,' I said as she brushed her teeth. 'I've been thinking. How about we don't go home quite yet?'

'Mum! Really?' She looked up at me, all big unblinking eyes.

'I think so, Emmie. We're not ready to go back yet, are we? How about another six months?'

'Yes, Mum, yes! Thank you!' We high-fived with happiness that our big adventure was still going.

CHAPTER 12

Nowhere but somewhere

I'd decided we would cross back into Vietnam on foot at a border crossing I'd heard was near Mondulkiri. I was tired of flying everywhere and wanted to do a bit more dirty travelling on buses and the roads less travelled. I wanted to crawl under the skin of Cambodia and make our way overland into Vietnam. We were both excited by what was ahead, not just now, but for the next six months. We were happy after our time with the elephants, and we were ready to roll into a challenge. A border-crossing adventure.

Even though I couldn't find much information online about the crossing, I was sure it would work. We had multi-entry Vietnam visas, so we could definitely get back in overland. I knew that the border was near a town called Snoul, and I just needed to find a bus to take us there. I spoke with the Khmer wife of the Aussie owner of the cafe in Sen Monorom, and she called a minivan driver who was going to Phnom Penh the next day. We were hopeful that he would drop us off at Snoul, but if not, it would be on the turn-off, so we could make our way there … somehow.

Emmie and I needed to be at the cafe at 8.00 am the next morning. We were ready for this.

'You know, Emmie, when we walk across the border, we will be in a place called no man's land,' I told her. 'It's not Cambodia and it's not Vietnam. It's the middle of nowhere.'

'So, what if we just stayed there? No one can get us. If I was a robber and people wanted to catch me, I would just put up a tent and stay,' she said.

'Ha! I like your thinking, Emmie. I'm not sure how that would work, but you are one sneaky little girl,' I laughed.

That morning, I had the easiest packing of our entire trip. We'd only brought our daypacks with us and had hardly anything in them. Carrying around a big backpack was driving me nuts, and even though we didn't carry much with us, it always seemed to grow. While I didn't mind the pack being heavy—and, to be honest, I never had to carry it too far—the pack explosions got me down. Minutes after I unzipped it, its entire contents were all over the room. Every time we moved, I was literally repacking the pack.

First, I'd pack up all the items in their little packing cubes, the undies and cossies in one, medicine and toiletries in another. Then a cube for my clothes and a cube for Emmie's clothes, then the big blue folders of schoolwork. Then Emmie's toys, our snorkels and masks, a little bag of chargers, the GoPro and our shoes were all shoved in. Emmie had usually filled her daypack with junk, and there was no more room in it, so I needed to put her things into the big pack—colouring books, toys, playdough … and then there were my books (until I bought a Kindle and saved space and weight), and I had a folder of random stuff such as ticket stubs and notes, a world map … it was ridiculous!

I usually ended up carrying the backpack, two daypacks and a shoulder bag a lot of the time, and it all would get pretty heavy. For a while, we carried two ukuleles as well. How crazy! We never even tried to play these ukuleles—not even once—and we carried them all over Asia for a few months. I really wanted to learn … I guess there's still time.

People often ask what souvenirs we collected on our travels, and the answer is none apart from the occasional stable of soft toys Emmie would gather, or the rocks and sticks I would find hidden in pockets. If Emmie wanted something, my answer was mostly 'It won't fit in the backpack.' And I had the same response when something caught my eye, too. The one exception was Blair the Penguin, a soft toy given to Emmie by the lovely Aitara at the Westin Hotel in Hangzhou. That penguin spent almost two years with us on the road, and was sneakily replaced once when she was left at Beijing Airport. When you're carrying your life on your back, there's not much room to add physical memories, and Emmie and I would often find something we wanted and say, 'I'd love to get this but … it won't fit in the backpack.' That was our test. If I could squish it in, then maybe. But mostly we went without because … it woudn't fit in the backpack!

That morning packing up in Sen Monorom was so easy. I simply packed up two little daypacks, and off we walked down the street to the cafe and, hopefully, a border-crossing bus pick-up. We sat down on the wooden benches, had a quick breakfast and then waited … and waited … and waited. A couple of Aussie blokes rocked up and were waiting, too, which was reassuring.

It gave me hope that we would get there. Finally, the little minivan pulled up and we all climbed aboard. It was quite full, with tourists and locals and a few British girls with beers in their hands at 9.00 am. Backpacker life! Those were the days, but it seemed very out of place in this soft, animist part of the world.

Stuffed beneath us were supplies being taken to villages along the way. We softly rested our feet on hessian bags and carefully manouevred around boxes of eggs and bags of grain. Life was under us as we bumped along, all hopeful of heading to the border. After a few hours and a few pit stops, the bus pulled up and the driver turned to us.

'Okay!' he said happily.

Luckily, there were so many of us crossing the border that the bus had taken us all the way to the Snoul crossing. It was just ahead, past a few buildings scattered along the dusty roadside. Emmie and I quickly jumped off the bus with our packs, took a punt on which building was immigration and made our way towards a window. I wanted to get ahead of the busload, and with only our daypacks, we were fast. I'd read that once we'd crossed the border we'd have to get motorbike taxis for about twenty kilometres to reach Lộc Ninh bus station in Vietnam. From there, we could find a bus to take us to Saigon. There were a few moving parts, and I had no idea how many motorbikes there would be, or if they'd all have helmets, so I didn't want to be last in the queue for a ride.

We'd guessed correctly, and we stood in the sun at the little window while an official checked our passports and visas. It was nerve-racking, and I felt a huge sense of relief when our passports were stamped. Off we walked across the red, dusty ground towards Vietnam. We left Cambodia and walked across no man's land between the two borders.

For about half a kilometre, we were nowhere.

And I'd never felt more strongly that I was somewhere.

Emmie powered ahead in her rainbow backpacker pants, thongs and hat, carrying her blue daypack and looking every bit the vagabond child. She was so confident but, more than that, just so accepting of the world and that today we would be crossing a border on foot. She was so happy with this adventurous life.

On the other side of no man's land, we entered a modern building and we were in Vietnam. Our bags were scanned, our visas checked and passports stamped, and then we walked out the doors to see a bunch of men with motorbikes.

This was going to be another first. We usually don't ride motorbikes—I've seen too many accidents and I don't feel like it's safe for Emmie—but since there was no other option, this was it. My only non-negotiable was helmets—we had to have them. I asked, and one of the Vietnamese men rustled up two helmets for us. Hooray! We climbed on the back of the bikes and set off into town for around $10 each.

'This is my baby,' I said to Emmie's driver. 'Very slow, very careful, okay?' He smiled, and I knew he would take care of her. Emmie wrapped her arms around his waist, and I prayed that she wouldn't let go and fly off the back. Off we went up the two-lane road and into town.

'Woooh, Emmie,' I yelled as we rode along the bumpy road.

'This is awesome,' she yelled back, and my heart just burst with pride at my adventurous little girl.

The drivers were super careful, and it was an easy ten-minute trip, much less than what we'd thought. It was the perfect end to our overland crossing, and it made me feel alive. The men dropped us at the bus stop, which was a small shop on the main road of town. We bought tickets for the bus to Saigon, used the toilet, grabbed some snacks and waited. Slowly, the other backpackers came dribbling in on the backs of bikes, and the bus eventually turned up, too. It was another minivan, with ducks under the seats and produce everywhere, and we drove along potholed roads, past temples and hawker markets and the dusty grit of real life.

Three hours later, we arrived in Saigon. We were stinky and dirty, and rewarded ourselves for navigating the overland border successfully with an overnight stay at the Sofitel. Ahhh, luxury! We had long baths and then set out in the steamy air to wander the streets. We walked quickly and directly across the busy roads as swarms of bikes poured around us. Crossing the street here can be scary and intimidating, but we had a little experience from a few busy intersections in Hội An. The trick is to keep moving, and the bikes will go around you. If you try to dodge them, it causes chaos. We kept our stride consistent and stepped off into the street, safely making it across every time. We wandered down the pretty Book Street, covered in golden fairy lights, to the famous Saigon Central Post Office and the pink Notre-Dame Cathedral before returning to the Sofitel for room-service burgers in bed and a peaceful sleep between crisp white sheets.

The next day, we flew back to Hội An and its lantern-lit streets, pho and *banh mi*, rice paddies, beaches and our room at our little guesthouse and friends all around us. It was so good to be home.

I checked my emails and saw one from the travel insurance company I used. It told me that I hadn't renewed my insurance. *Um, what?* I looked up my policy and saw that it had expired two months ago. *OH. MY. GOD.* We had been roaming around uninsured? When we went over the waterfall on a zipline, we were uninsured. When we were on the back of motorbikes in the middle of nowhere in Vietnam, we were uninsured. Not to mention Cambodia, China and all the flights and public transport. We were so lucky nothing had happened to us. I had to pay closer attention to my emails. I found a company who insured people already out of the country and sorted it out, and then kept it to myself. No one needed to know my latest stuff-up.

We settled back into the days we both enjoyed. The little special moments in Hội An still make me smile, like the day Mr Vu the computer repairman sent a man on a bike to collect my broken Mac. This bloke just walked into the cafe, told me Mr Vu had sent him, put my laptop under his arm and rode off into the traffic. True to Mr Vu's word, the laptop came back in perfect condition three days later.

My back had been seizing up and giving me pain for a while, and I wanted to see someone about it. I found a doctor who practised traditional Chinese medicine way out in the Hội An 'burbs, and I was pretty keen to see him to get my back fixed. After cracking me all over, he wanted to do some acupuncture and stuck needles in my bum. Then he attached electrodes to them and turned on the power. OMG! There was a current going through my bum.

'Emmie, quick, check where the wires are going to,' I hissed, scared he had connected me to the mains and a power surge might blow me up. It was not my plan to be electrocuted in my bum with my skirt pulled up in a stranger's home in Hội An. Emmie followed the wires for me.

'It's okay, Mum, it's just a small box,' she said. Phew.

Mum arrived for a couple of weeks and happened to be with us on my birthday. I wanted to do something special, so at the last minute we decided to fly to Siem Reap. She had never been to

Cambodia, and I wanted to watch the sunrise over the temples of Angkor with Mum and Emmie after another loop around the sun.

We stayed in luxury at the beautiful Anantara Angkor Resort and set out to the temples before dawn on my birthday to spend my first morning of my new year at one of my favourite places. I stood in front of Angkor Wat with Mum, Emmie asleep on a sarong on the ground in front of us. Slowly, a hot red pinprick of sun rose into the dusty sky, and a soft golden glow surrounded the temple. This moment was everything. Emmie woke up and put her arm around me, and Mum was standing right by my side. I was so emotional because I felt so content, and feeling content was strange.

When you always feel like you should be striving for something more, simply being satisfied can seem like not enough. After always struggling for something in my life, and especially after the challenges of the past few years, I was unfamiliar with such an internal calmness, a feeling of just being, not needing to be anywhere or an urgency to do something. I was just me and I was happy right where I was, content and satisfied with what I had. This was what I needed in my life. It was like I'd found the secret to my happiness.

I thought back to my birthday a year before, when my eardrum had exploded and we'd only been on the road for three weeks. So much had happened since then, and I'd changed so much, learned so much and was so grateful. I'd got my wish to be with Emmie, and I'd found peace. I wasn't ready to change that, not when I'd finally found what I was looking for ... which was ... nothing. As long as I had Emmie by my side, I was happy to just be.

The next weekend was all for me. With Mum in town, I got a break and had my first girls' weekend in more than a year. Jacqui flew in from Singapore and we met up in Saigon, staying at the landmark Caravelle Saigon hotel, where Australian news crews lived and reported during the Vietnam War. We wandered the streets, lay by the pool drinking beer and reading books, and spent Sunday at the InterContinental's free-flow champagne brunch, devouring fresh seafood and unlimited Bollinger. Luckily it was just across the road from the Caravelle, so we could snooze the afternoon away.

Back in Hội An, I doubled Mum all around town on my bike like a buffalo dragging its load. She sat on the padded seat on the back, waving regally and bestowing *xin chao* greetings to locals and tourists like she was royalty.

'Mum, are you serious?' I laughed at her as I dragged us up a hill, my legs burning and lungs puffing while she *xin chao*'d from her bike-throne. 'You're not the bloody queen of Vietnam! Give it a rest.'

She loved it back there, except on the day she wore her wide-legged pants that got caught in my back wheel and nearly amputated her leg.

'Stop, stop!' she screamed as I heard a strange grinding noise and it became harder to pedal. I stopped and turned to see her half off the bike, pants ripped to her bum.

'Oh my God, Mum! Are you kidding me?' I laughed and laughed. 'You're lucky you didn't lose your leg!'

Two Vietnamese shopkeepers raced over to help us. One cut Mum's pants out of the wheel and prised her from the bike, the other put the bike chain back on. Mum released, we crossed the road to buy her a new pair of pants from one of the ubiquitous Hội An clothes shops, but she wasn't happy. Those wide-legged pants had been her favourites.

'Well, you're lucky you still have two legs,' I told her. 'Get back on, and keep your pants away from the wheel this time!' God, she is hilarious.

And then Mum flew back to Sydney, and it was just Emmie and me again, settled into our Hội An home until our next move. We had no plans and nowhere to be. What to do?

'Your choice, Emmie,' I said. 'Make it a good one.'

CHAPTER 13

Emmie's choice

'Mummy, I've made my decision for our next adventure,' Emmie announced one afternoon in March. 'I want to walk on the glass in China! Can we go?'

'Sure, why not?' I told her. 'I said it was your choice, and you've picked somewhere awesome! Good one, Emmie.'

She'd chosen for us to go to Zhangjiajie to explore the glass walkway around the top of Tianmen Mountain. Emmie had become obsessed after watching videos of people freaking out and hugging the side of the mountain as they inched along the walkway. It looked challenging and fun, and incredibly beautiful.

Vietnam was moving into its peak of heat and humidity, and we had two weeks left on our visa before we needed to leave our spirit town. China seemed like a good idea, and so we would continue our irrational path of squiggles and right angles across Asia. We had a visit left on our multi-entry China visa that was about to expire, and I loved it when Emmie got excited about a new place to visit. Everything came together—this trip was meant to be, and we couldn't wait.

My friend Jenny, who was now working for a not-for-profit organisation in Saigon, visited us in Hội An for a weekend. As we worked on our laptops by the pool at Sunrise Resort, where I'd joined the gym for a cheap monthly rate and also got to use the pool and kids' club, I told her about our plan.

'Want to come to China?' I asked. 'It's seriously one of our favourite places, and these mountains look unreal. There's a glass walkway, a glass elevator, and those amazing mountains that were in the movie *Avatar*. April is supposed to be a good time to visit.' (As it turned out, it wasn't. Ha.)

Jenny was in. We spent the rest of the afternoon figuring out how to get there. Emmie and I loved to take the train, but it seemed like a bit of a mission, so we splashed out on flights and started booking guesthouses.

It wasn't easy to figure out where to stay or how to get around the mountains. There was hardly any information online, so we just hoped for the best. Jenny was in organiser mode, and I was happy to leave it to her. In fact, I was super happy to not be leading the way for a change.

And then we were off again! We packed up our backpacks and farewelled our Hội An friends. It was always easy coming and going from Hội An. Hellos and goodbyes were pretty casual, and we were fairly sure we would see our friends again, back in Hội An or somewhere else.

We flew down to Saigon to meet Jenny, then caught a China Southern flight to Shenzen and a China Eastern flight to Zhangjiajie. It was a bumpy 90-minute flight, and strange sounds kept me on edge. After more than twelve months of flying, I was no better at being in the air. I had a constant internal monologue that detected and assessed aircraft sounds, angles of turns, elevation and proximity to land, other aircraft and mountains. Clearly, I am not qualified to assess flight safety and question any movements, but that doesn't stop me. I often freak out about how close we are to other planes, only to realise that I'm staring at our own wing lights. I constantly scan the faces of flight attendants for glimpses of uncertainty or terror, just in case we are about to crash.

We grabbed a taxi, showing the driver my phone with the screenshot of the Zhangjiajie Yijiaqin Hotel guesthouse address in Mandarin. The accommodation was cheap and the rooms were big, with a queen bed and a large bathroom with generous shower and hot water. Our window looked out over a neighbour's garden and distant mountains. We were on the third floor, and our door opened straight onto a tiled staircase, so early-morning wake-ups from clattering feet and chattering Chinese tourists were the norm. We loved it and would lie in bed, smiling.

We met Jenny the next morning after she had spent two hours walking around the town, investigating while we'd been lazing in bed.

'Um, did you know it's a Chinese holiday?' she asked me. She'd been downstairs talking to our host, Rocky, one of the nicest blokes and another amazingly helpful host. 'It's so crowded, and the lines are so long!'

'Ha, of course it is. Oh well, what's another couple of million people on the mountain?' I laughed. I wasn't surprised. Of course we'd landed in a popular Chinese tourist area on a public-holiday weekend. Chinese holidays are almost impossible for tourists, because they are just so busy. I know I'd said when we first started out that I would this stuff, but we weren't planning on exploring until the next day anyway. We could wait it out.

'Let's just see how we go. Maybe it's not that bad, and if the holiday ends on Monday, there won't be so many people going up the mountain,' I suggested.

Jenny's and my styles of travel were so different. She's an organiser who loves having a strict plan, and I'm the opposite, with my unplanned, disorganised go-with-the-flow ways. I'm sure it was frustrating for her, but it was good for me to have someone else at the wheel. We decided to take the world's biggest cable car up the Tianmen Mountain on Monday to the glass walkway, but Jenny had been out sleuthing around the cable-car station and reckoned the line just to buy the tickets was hours long. Rocky came to the rescue.

'Give me your passports and money, and my friend will queue for you at 2.00 am and bring your tickets here,' he told us. Back in the day, I would never have handed over my passport, but Rocky seemed cool and I couldn't be bothered to line up myself. We handed everything over and left it to someone else to do the hard yards for us. When Jacqui and I were backpacking, we would never have paid an extra $3 for this service, either. What fools we were! One of the best lessons I learned on this trip is that there is nothing wrong with paying a little extra to make life easier.

The next morning, our tickets arrived thanks to Rocky and his mate, and we set off for the world's biggest cable car, walking along the roadside through the grey, misty town and joining the queue.

Chinese efficiency meant that within minutes we were sailing up the side of the mountain on our way to the glass walkway.

At the top, pathways ran in all directions, and we followed one the meandered along the cliff-top. Around a corner, we spotted the glass walkway, clear and fragile-looking as it clung to the mountain, 1.4 kilometres above the ground.

'Mum, Mum! Here it is,' yelled Emmie, grabbing my hand and dragging me towards it. 'Let's go!'

We walked down a set of stairs to the walkway entrance. The queue was much smaller than I'd expected, and we grabbed booties from a tub, put them on and began walking across the glass, looking down to the winding 99 Bend Road and scrubby ground below. It was a mental game. I had to remind myself that we'd just been walking on the same walkway around the other side of the mountain, the only difference was that it had a solid floor. With a clear floor, everyone just freaked out. Emmie was loving watching the people clinging to the side of the mountain and sliding their way across inch by inch as she danced on the glass.

There was so much to see up in the mountains, with incredible surprises around every corner, such as the little chairlifts that crisscrossed from peak to peak, and the mind-blowing Bailong glass elevator in Wulingyuan Scenic Area. It looked like it was straight out of Willy Wonka's chocolate factory, an actual glass elevator that shot straight up the side of the mountain, 32 storeys high. When we arrived at the top, the fog cleared for a minute and we had an amazing view of jagged, tree-covered golden shards striking up into the sky. Then we took twenty sets of escalators back down through the rocky core of the mountain. It was just incredible.

We left Rocky and moved to a guesthouse in the Wulingyuan area for a few nights. The family had just converted their home, and we were the first-ever guests. The owners were so sweet, and we could tell they'd gone to a lot of effort with what they had to make their home welcoming. The rooms were tidy and clean, and the bathroom had a squatter, so Emmie was happy. There was a small trail to a lookout that they'd made themselves, carving a path into the side of the mountain. The view was spectacular. We had a fabulous meal, home-cooked by one of the men, and we communicated via a translate app. The hostess, Qantanqai, told me, 'This is our house, but we are residents of the mountain.' My heart.

The Avatar Hallelujah Mountain was covered in fog every day we were there, and it was so disappointing. We moved to another guesthouse on the other side of the mountains, the beautiful No 5 Valley Inn, and each day while Jenny was hiking around, Emmie and I would take a cable car up to the mountains and be greeted with a wall of thick white cloud that never went away.

The Wulingyuan area was so well organised, with looping shuttles, food stalls and signs in Chinese and English. We walked around the huge shards of mountains, and watched men carrying Chinese tourists up the hill on bamboo thrones.

'Please, Mum, can I have a go?' begged Emmie. Business looked slow, and I felt for these men trying to earn an income. We negotiated a ride, and Emmie was carried up the hill on a little throne on top of two bamboo poles. She loved it, and we were all laughing as I tried to race them. At the top of the mountain, Emmie and I looked out over the fog and decided that instead of taking the cable car, we would hike down the mountain, hoping that as we did the fog might clear a little.

We walked down a steep track around the side of the mountain, stopping at little lookouts and walls of rock covered in pretty green moss. Two hours later, we finally reached the bottom. We popped out from the little path we'd been following onto a walkway and, strangely, the two men who had carried Emmie in the bamboo chair were standing in front of us. We were so confused and all just stared at each other. Wait …

'We're still at the top of the mountain, Emmie! How did that happen?' I couldn't understand it. Surely we had been walking down the mountain? How did we end up back at the top?

'Well, I'm not trying to walk down again, Mum,' said Emmie. 'Let's get the cable car.'

After all our time on the road, my sense of direction still hadn't improved.

In the mountains, a series of shuttle buses looped around to lookouts and hikes, and it was easy to catch them—unless a mob of hundreds of tourists suddenly appeared, as they did with us. We did a bad thing here. I felt terrible afterwards, and I will never do it again … but … we queue-jumped. It was just that we'd spent three days up on the mountain waiting for the fog to clear, and it was almost impossible to see the shards. I was racing to try to get to a viewing spot and, well … I made Emmie pretend she had twisted her ankle so we could get to the front of the line. I'd never done this before. I've never pretended that Emmie was younger than she was to pay less, and I've never pushed in. I am not a pusher. But I crossed the line to the dark side, and the Chinese, Japanese and Korean tourists kindly let us in, and even offered Emmie heat pads for her injury. Taking advantage of people's kindness was not a nice feeling. We both felt really bad. We did get to the front, and then we got to see more fog, hoping that no one noticed Emmie's miraculous recovery.

We were still waiting for the fog to move yet again when a message from our guesthouse in Yangshuo popped up on my phone, asking where we were. It seemed that we were supposed to have arrived that morning but instead we were sitting on the mountain, hundreds of kilometres away. *Oops.* We'd missed our overnight train and our pick-up. This was why we didn't usually book in advance!

We said goodbye to Jenny, raced back down the mountain to Zhangjiajie and, with Rocky's help, we bought new tickets on the overnight train to Guilin via Changsha. Rocky made sure we had the correct tickets, and our compartment in the soft sleeper carriage had a door. A door! We were so happy. We had curtains on the windows, soft doonas and pillows on the beds, plus a kettle and small metal tin on a little table.

'This is Chinese train luxury!' said Emmie.

'Welcome to your private carriage, madam,' I told her.

There were three levels of bunks, and the middle one was folded down to make a backrest so we could use the bottom bunks as seats until bedtime. We waited for someone to board and join our compartment, but no one did. It was all ours. Hooray!

Conductors in slick uniforms with stripes on the shoulders roamed the corridors, and the dining car was full of people eating, drinking and smoking as the train hurtled through the night. The only indication of our speed was our frequently popping ears and the wind that rushed down the hall when the carriage door opened.

We had the big backpack, two small daypacks and my shoulder bag, a bag of food, a bag of random items, the two ukuleles and Emmie's green *Monsters, Inc.* helmet strapped to the backpack.

The backpack had felt so much heavier as I dragged it up to the train, and as I unpacked and tried to rearrange everything, I realised that my cheapskate ways had added so much weight as I pulled out bottle after bottle of water from the No 5 Valley Inn. I took the bottles out and pushed everything I could into the big pack, then pulled and pulled the zipper, squeezing the sides together to close it.

RIIIIPPPPPPPPPPPPPPPPPPP.

Bloody hell. The side of the backpack had torn apart. Of course, I'd abused my twenty-year-old backpack until it had completely given up. Now I'd have to hunt down a seamstress when we got to Yangshuo, as well as a heavy-duty laundry to clean our disgusting clothes. I bound up the pack as best I could using its straps, and we spread our sleeping sheets out on our beds and slept until 4.45 am.

We arrived at Changsha at around 5.00 am and discovered that we needed to get the train to Yangshuo from an entirely different train station on the other side of the city. As we emerged from the station, we walked into a cluster of private drivers hoping to get a fare. Among all the men was one woman and, after negotiating, we walked over to her old car and jumped in, motoring down the freeway in the dark to the next station. We spoke a little and found that to try to earn an income for her family, this woman would get up at 4.00 am each day to meet this train, hoping to get a fare before she went to work. It wasn't the safest job, and a fare wasn't even guaranteed. Again, I was reminded of how hard people work to care for their families.

My eyes caught sight of something ahead of us on the freeway and I couldn't figure out what it was. It looked like huge chunks of paper slowly rising from the middle of the freeway, floating up into the air and elegantly twisting and turning in the sky. It was hypnotic, and my brain couldn't understand what was happening until, suddenly, a white car burst into view, out of control and hurtling towards us. I'd been watching the dividers from the highway being flung up into the air as the car drove into them. It crossed over to our side of the road, hurtled in front of us, a whisper of air between us, and slammed into the side of the freeway.

'Oh my God!' I screamed, looking behind me to see the car crumpled against the wall. Our driver started chanting and shaking, and turned to look at me, huge eyes wide with shock. She kept driving, and I thought to myself that we should stop, but what could we do? Someone else would have to stop, we couldn't turn on the freeway and our driver was freaking out. We didn't know if the other driver was okay. What had happened?

Two seconds. That's all it would have taken. If they'd been two seconds slower, if we'd been two seconds faster, we would have been right in the car's path. Someone was watching out for us, I was certain.

Another train station, another train and then we were off to Yangshuo and a place I'd been hanging out to get to—the Yangshuo Mountain Retreat, a gorgeous guesthouse on the banks of the Yulong River, nestled below the stunning limestone mountains.

As soon as we arrived, Yangshuo's spirit town vibes hit me with a whack of love in my heart and a shiver down my spine. It was the vibe, the feeling of being home, of being at peace and also a feeling of joy. I'd love to find out more about my Asian spirit towns: Penang, Siem Reap, Hội An and, now, Yangshuo. Maybe it's just me, or maybe there is something about the location, or the people or just some earthly goodness that seeps up into the air and permeates everything. Emmie feels it, too. There are places that made us feel good and alive and happy, and Yangshuo was one of these.

We settled into the Yangshuo Mountain Retreat (where they kindly arranged to have our pack sewn up), and I scoffed some Sichuan chicken while Emmie had a toasted sandwich and we watched people pass by on bamboo rafts. We had to do it, too, and it wasn't long before we were on a raft floating down the Yulong River. We sat on little chairs with water lapping at our feet through the bamboo floor, and Emmie wore a flower crown we'd bought from an elderly lady as we walked along the riverside. A young bloke guided us with a bamboo pole, and we floated down small rapids, past the green karst mountains and children playing on the riverbank. It was heaven.

We spent a wonderful few days in Yangshuo. We watched a musical in the natural limestone amphitheatre and cried from the beauty and emotion of hundreds of local people performing with passion. We went to the Gold Water Cave and walked through the huge limestone caverns with formations lit up by kitschy coloured lights. Judgmental previous me would have turned my nose up, but now I enjoyed this uniquely Chinese display, and Emmie thought it was beautiful. We ended our tour sliding down a natural rock slippery dip into metre-deep cold mud, rinsing off in the hot spring right next to it.

We cycled through fields and along tiny dirt paths, and were punted across the river by men on their bamboo rafts. We climbed Moon Hill and ate fresh strawberries bought from a roadside stall. Yangshuo is the only place where I cried when we left. I felt torn from this gorgeous spot, my ultimate spirit town. It was one of the highlights of our trip, and we radiated happiness.

We were given first-class seats on the train back to Shenzen, either by accident or because I accidentally bought the wrong ones. Probably the latter, with my track record. Transport is so punctual in China that we made it to the airport right on time for our flight to Kuala Lumpur. We touched down at midnight and spent the next six hours in the airport's Starbucks Hotel waiting for our connection.

At 6.00 am, I rolled sleeping Emmie from the Starbucks couch onto the luggage trolley, laid her over the packs and wheeled her and our bags to the Air Asia counter to check in for our flight to Colombo, Sri Lanka. Another adventure was just beginning.

CHAPTER 14

Open doors

Sri Lanka had lovely memories for me. Twenty years before, I'd travelled solo around the country and then met up with George on its southern coast. I could still picture us on the beach at Unawatuna, young, happy and carefree. I love how travel transports me not only physically, but also emotionally, and remembering those days made me smile. Travelling with kids is awesome, but those long-ago days of child-free backpacking were idyllic. There's so much freedom travelling with kids, but it's freedom with responsibility. Backpacking when you're young is an experience that can't be replicated with little ones in tow.

On the plane from Kuala Lumpur to Colombo, a toddler popped her head up from the seat in front and started playing with Emmie, and I started chatting with her parents. Olive's mum

Carlie was from rural Victoria, and her dad Sarana was Sri Lankan. They were on their way to see his family in Kandy. Emmie and I were heading that way, too, and they kindly offered to take us in their car. We jumped at the offer, too tired to find the bus to the train station and wait in 40-degree heat for four hours for our train. We chatted all the way to Kandy and stayed in touch on Facebook. It was nice to have a local contact, just in case we needed a hand.

We'd been travelling for around sixteen months when we arrived in Sri Lanka. The lack of time to myself, concerns about money and nonstop responsibility were starting to get me down. Plus, I was trying to teach Emmie again, which meant we were arguing and I was getting tired of it. All of a sudden, I was finding it difficult to back my own decisions, second-guessing myself and being short tempered and grumpy.

What was bugging me at the time was money—or lack of it. I loved the way we had travelled, it had been easy in part because we didn't have a strict budget to stick to. I tried to keep us mostly low spending, staying in hostels and cheap guesthouses, and eating local and riding public transport. But if Emmie or I wanted to do something, we did it, and our dwindling funds reflected that. My savings were getting low, and they were all the cash I had; I didn't want to hit the bottom. I knew we'd have to head home soon so I could top up.

The guesthouse we'd booked in Kandy was questionable at best. It was reasonably clean but far out of town, and young men were lounging around on the couches in tracksuit pants, playing on their phones. I didn't want to stay, so we decided to head north for a bit. We grabbed a tuk tuk to the bus station, roamed around and found a minibus to Dambulla, grabbed some *pakoras* and vegetable pastries at one of the shops, and jumped on. I looked up accommodation in Sigiriya while we were on the road and found a guesthouse called The Hideout that looked amazing, if a little out of our budget. I booked us in for a few nights, and once off the bus at Dambulla, we grabbed another tuk tuk to Sigiriya and our little $60-a-night paradise.

'Mum! Look at the pool! Let's swim, Mum, come on!' Emmie yelled as we arrived. We raced up to our room to change.

We fell in love with this gorgeous guesthouse built with love by a beautiful family. The rooms surrounded a big swimming pool, and there were handmade treehouses and platforms, showers shaped like elephants, and vine-covered doorways. Its restaurant made delicious Sri Lankan dishes and served buffalo curd and honey for dessert. We planned an early-morning assault on Sigiriya—the Lion Rock—followed by an elephant safari at Minneriya National Park, about 40 minutes north, and spent the afternoon in the pool.

The next morning, we were up early to climb to the top of the ancient rock fortress at Sigiriya. It reminded me a little of Uluru, jutting 200 metres out of the flat earth, red and rusty. Climbing it wasn't as hard as it looked, thank goodness. We walked through some of the oldest landscaped gardens in the world, up staircases and past moats and rock murals. Then came the final ascent, past the huge carved Lion's Paw and up a narrow staircase to the top and the stunning ancient palace ruins. It's hard to comprehend how the palace was built up there, and how the workers and monks managed to make it up rickety ladders attached to the side of the steep rock.

After lunch, we were picked up by a couple of young blokes in a jeep for our elephant safari. It cost us $50, and we had the whole jeep to ourselves. There were a bunch of other jeeps at Minneriya, and we entered the park together, driving on rocky roads and stopping almost straight away to peer through the trees at a family of elephants mooching around the bush.

I was a bit annoyed with our driver, as I felt that he didn't give us enough time to look at these elephants and moved on too quickly, passing by another couple of elephants I could see through the trees. I tapped on the glass window between us, got his attention and asked if he would please stop so we could look at them. Emmie and I were both feeling very emotional and happy, and we wanted to see more of these incredible creatures. I couldn't understand why he was moving so quickly, and I was getting grumpy with him.

He just smiled, and suddenly we drove around a corner to a huge open plain, and Emmie and I burst into tears. In front of us were hundreds of elephants wandering in the grass and playing in the ancient reservoir. They roamed together, guarding their little ones, playing, running and hanging out under the blue sky, happy and free. It was the most amazing and unexpected sight I'd ever seen.

This was how we needed to see them, just elephants being elephants in the wild. It caught our hearts, and we spent hours watching them.

Driving back to The Hideout, Emmie screamed and grabbed my arm. 'No! Mummy, look, the elephant has chains on,' she cried, tears on her cheeks. We stopped the jeep and got out to see the elephant. Her owner came to us to offer us a ride.

'I would never ride your beautiful elephant,' said Emmie softly. 'Why can't you let her free?'

'It is my income,' he answered. 'But you can buy her for US$18,000.'

This poor elephant was standing on dirt under the shade of the small tree she was tied to. Her skin was mottled, and she stood swaying while only a few kilometres away, other elephants were free to play and live a wild life.

'We have to tell people not to ride elephants, Mum,' Emmie said. And she did. We made a little video and shared it on our Facebook and Instagram pages. I loved that she was becoming passionate about the things she was seeing and thinking of ways to raise awareness.

The next day, we caught a tuk tuk to Dambulla to get a bus back to Kandy. There were no seats, so Emmie sat on the console right next to the driver while I stood. As we drove on, the kind Sri Lankan people rearranged themselves like a puzzle to make room for Emmie on a seat, and she slotted in. We bumped along in an audio soup of blaring pop music from the driver's radio, videos with information about how to deal with wild elephants on roadways playing on the TV, and horns honking at us as we rattled along the rickety road.

In Kandy, we grabbed a tuk tuk to our next accommodation, an old run-down colonial house with stunning views over the mountains and city. We had an early start the next day for a ride on the blue train to the mountains of Ella. Sitting in train doorways when I was exploring Sri Lanka alone all those years before was one of my favourite memories of that trip. I was so looking forward to sharing the doorway-hang magic with Emmie. But first I had to get us tickets.

Getting train tickets can be a bit tricky in Sri Lanka, especially since the blue train route between Kandy and Ella is such an iconic trip. They go on sale 30 days in advance and generally sell out quickly. There were no tickets left for our train, but we were going to try to get two of the few that were sold on the day by queuing super early at the ticket counter. In fact, we went one better, after a couple of backpackers we were chatting to during a cultural dance performance that afternoon suggested driving twenty minutes away to the next town, which was non-touristy, so we could buy our tickets quickly without having to queue.

We followed their advice early the next morning and *voila*! There was no one else at the ticket window at Peradeniya, and we got our tickets within minutes. We returned to Kandy and saw people still queuing, but we had our tickets! We bought some short eats—curry puffs, savoury pastries and bread—and water for our ride. I couldn't wait to get on. We stowed our pack in the overhead rack and checked our seats. We were ready to go.

'Come on, Emmie, let's sit in the doorway,' I said with a huge smile as the train slowly moved out of town. I couldn't wait to share this with her.

'In the doorway, Mum?' I'd spoken to her about the joy of doorway hangs, but I don't think she'd believed me. I couldn't wait to get our spot and just sit.

We wandered to the vestibule at the end of the carriage, pulled open the heavy door and sat down next to each other, thongs off and stashed behind us, bums on the carriage floor and feet hanging below. We held on to the smooth silver handrails as the hypnotic beat of the wheels clicking over the tracks filled our heads and vibrated through our bodies and we gazed out over the bush, green paddies, palms, waterfalls and mountains. We passed villages and locals waiting alongside the tracks for the train to pass—children in school uniforms, women in bright, colourful saris and men in their traditional loose pants. We watched women picking leaves in tea plantations that grew up mountainsides and passed through old white train stations with colonial architecture and names painted in a distinctive black font. Long, golden weeds whipped our feet, and we bought peanuts and samosas from local men who sold them as the train sped between stations, the food wrapped in their children's handwritten pages of homework.

It was serene, it was peaceful, it was everything I needed to calm my churning mind.

We sat in the doorway of the train for hours, only moving to let others have a turn and jumping back in when they were done. We wrapped our arms around each other, held hands, and Emmie rested her head against my shoulder as we reminisced about our trip. We knew that we would have to pop home soon. We would go home, work and save, and we would be off again. It made sense in theory, but every single cell in my body said no.

One of my biggest worries was that if we went home, I might revert into the old me, trying to be someone else to fit in. Would I feel sad about what we didn't have in comparison to other people, while right now I spent every single day full of joy at the abundance of our life? What about work? How would I cope going back into the city each day and hardly seeing Emmie?

And how would Emmie be? I didn't want her to conform either. I had so much to consider. We were so happy and free right now. I didn't want to go back. I would shake and my heart would race in panic just thinking about it. We would go home, but not just yet. It wasn't time.

'I love this. MUM, I LOVE IT,' Emmie roared with delight as she sat in the doorway, her hair blowing in the wind.

And then in quiet times, holding hands. 'This is my best place, here with you, Mama.'

Sri Lanka had that effect on us. It was getting into our bones. The tropical heat, the dust and the beautiful greens of the palm trees and the rice paddies were making me feel close to the world again.

In Ella, the laidback hippie town covered with twinkling fairy lights, we climbed Little Adam's Peak and walked through tea plantations to the Nine Arch Bridge at Demodara, where we watched the blue train cross while we drank fresh juice at a tiny shop on the side of the mountain. We walked the tracks back to Ella with school kids and the occasional cow, and practised jumping off the tracks quickly in case of an approaching train.

Later, we were inside a little glass box withdrawing money from the ATM in the main street when we heard a rustling noise and then a friendly voice filled the booth.

'Hello, little baby,' it said. 'Please take off your hat.'

'Emmie, take off your hat! It's security!'

Emmie quickly took off her hat, and then . . .

'Hello, little baby,' the voice said again. It was quickly joined by another.

'Are you having a good holiday?'

'Oh my gosh, Mum, they're real people!' laughed Emmie.

They were. It was hilarious. We looked at each other and started laughing, and Emmie was twirling around trying to find the camera, waving and giggling.

'Hello, hello,' she danced around the small glass box. 'Can you see me?'

It was so funny and such a little highlight of our day. I took my money out of the machine, and we turned to walk out the door.

'You have a good day,' the voices said. 'Bye bye, baby!'

It was time for the beach. A lady named Sarah messaged me on Instagram to tell us she was staying with her kids in Tangalle, but to head to Hiriketiya instead as the beach was small and beautiful. We tried to get a bus, but they pulled in to the station so quickly that by the time I'd run up to ask if they were headed to the coast, they were already moving out of the station again. I chased the buses for a little while and got nowhere, so I gave up and agreed to let the tuk tuk man who'd been hanging around take us all the way to the beach. It was a good three hours in the back, with Emmie sleeping on me until we arrived at the quiet and stunning horseshoe bay.

We had a beautiful time in Hiri. It was so laidback, peaceful and calm, and it had the most gorgeous little quirks. The bread man in his tuk tuk would rise over the hill with 'Greensleeves' playing on a loudspeaker, and we would run after him and buy our sweet bread rolls. In the evening, we would wander the streets, buying vegetable curry parcels and roti, and in the mornings, we'd watch flying peacocks flap from palm tree to palm tree as tribes of monkeys roamed the jungle.

We still needed to go home. It was on my mind, but I ignored it and I didn't book flights, and we carried on with our amazing adventures in Sri Lanka. Emmie learned to surf with Madhu, and we spent our days swimming and playing, and chasing the bread man barefoot down the street. We hung out with Marty, an Aussie who owned the Beach House guesthouse and cafe, his family and the few people who were at Hiri in the tail-end of the season, eating pizza and heading into the back streets for curry. I fell in love with Hiri and tried to buy a little parcel of land, but it didn't work out. It seemed to for many, many others, though, as this quiet little spot is now quite developed and popular. Everything changes so fast these days.

I resisted making the decision to go home for as long as I could, but I knew that we had to. My friend Jodie messaged me to say that she had a media role coming up for a few months if I wanted it, and it seemed that although my heart and mind said not to go, the universe was telling me that we needed to get back to Australia.

It all happened so quickly. It was the only way I could do it. I went onto Skyscanner and bought two tickets to Sydney for the next day. Then it was done, and I couldn't debate or resist it anymore. The feeling of going against everything my heart and body and mind was telling me to do was intense. At the same time, I knew that I was tired and we needed a break. We wouldn't have to stay at home for long. I would earn money, and then we could travel again. I told my mum and dad that we were coming home and asked to stay at their place for a bit. We packed up our bags and off we went home to Sydney, Australia.

We'd been gone for a year and seven months. Re-entry wouldn't be easy.

⌣

When we flew into Sydney, we went straight to Mum and Dad's place 'for a bit' ... and then kind of decided to stay there. It made sense. There was a school down the road that Emmie could go to for a few months, and we weren't planning on staying for long. Mum and Dad have a big house, and while we cramped their style, I know that they loved having Emmie around.

I went back into the exact lifestyle I'd so happily left. I would walk to the station at 6.30 am and get the train into the city, head to my desk and work all day. Then I'd leave work at around 5.30 pm and be home at around 7.30 pm, depending on the trains.

At first it was novel to be back, but I soon realised that I didn't have the drive I used to have for corporate work. I didn't care about the office politics, the painful approval processes and the in-house class system. I'd started earning a little money from putting advertising on my Instagram account and for paid blog posts. I was doing my own work on weekends and on the train each weekday, sitting in the quiet carriage and glaring at anyone who uttered a sound. My friends laughed and called me the Noise Ranger, and I took that role seriously, it was the only fun part of the working day. But I didn't want to work in the city. I'd been a corporate minion for twenty years, and I just didn't want to waste time anymore.

Two months in, I resigned. Jodie wasn't too happy with me and I didn't blame her, but one of the things I'd learned while I was away was to make decisions based on what was best for Emmie and me, and it was best for me to not be doing this. Over the past year and a half I'd spent every day with Emmie, and to go from that to hardly seeing her at all again was just too much. Finding balance remained the biggest challenge of all.

It was around this time that Carlie, who I'd met on the plane from Kuala Lumpur to Colombo, emailed me. She had started a travel business and wanted to share a couple of stories I'd posted on my blog about Sri Lanka. We started chatting, and I told her about my dream to run family holidays for solo mums. All of a sudden, we were planning one for Sri Lanka in January 2018. It was only a couple of months away, but I was confident that we could make it happen, and we started promoting it on my social media channels and getting bookings. It was so exciting to be planning a trip, and Emmie and I had spent enough time in Sri Lanka to be able to map out a cool little route that included the elephants, the blue train, Ella and the beaches, plus a whole lot more.

It was so great to have a plan. We had something to look forward to—an early January trip that would kick off another six months of travel for us. I spent my days working out of the local library and earning enough money to keep us afloat. I didn't have to pay rent to my parents, who kindly put us up, so that took the pressure off financially.

It was strange being home and figuring out friendships, too. In a way, coming back was a great leveller. Some of my friends clicked back in with no effort whatsoever, but others ... well, it just no longer worked, and that was okay. Recognising it was a relief, because it meant that I didn't have to pretend anymore, and I suppose neither did they. It's incredibly liberating to release friendships and to not feel badly about it. If I hadn't found my self-confidence while we were travelling, I would have been doing anything and everything to get back into the fold. As it was, I just kind of shrugged and moved on, no hard feelings.

All along our journey, I'd met some incredible people whose friendships I valued so much, and they filled any kind of void. And I guess friendships are a bit like a puzzle: you have to find the right pieces to fit, and only a few special pieces fit closely and fill the gaps. I had my friends from school, good friends in the Shire, some wonderful friends I'd met on Instagram such as Amber and her family, who had driven around Australia in their kombi van, and my friend Narelle from the Gold Coast, and so many other families and mums in Sydney and around the world. Luckily for me, Amber was just down the road from my parents, and we met and talked for hours and hours—when you connect with someone who really gets you, it's just so easy, isn't it? While some of my friendships had changed, I didn't feel a sense of loss. In fact, I felt great. I didn't have people in my life that I didn't fit with, and I didn't have to pretend or try to be someone I wasn't.

It wasn't easy being back, but I knew I just had to get through it. Every time I drove back to the Shire, I would panic and my heart would race. Every part of my body told me being back was wrong. It wasn't time. But I knew that it wouldn't be long before we would go again, and in the meantime, whenever I found cheap flights on Skyscanner I was compelled to book them, and we went to Disneyland, Queensland and Bali while we were home, spending the money I earned back at work. I needed to keep moving so that I wouldn't feel stuck.

I'd become much more confident while I was away, thank goodness. I was so thankful I'd learned to be strong. One day, I was lying in bed at Mum and Dad's when I got an alert from Facebook Messenger. A new message. I took a look, and my heart stopped. It was one of the girls who had made my life so sad and uncomfortable after Emmie's dad had left. One who had told people lies about me, and who'd looked at me with disdain and turned her back after I had said hello at the shops, leaving me confused and hurt. I remembered my heart skipping and my skin feeling hot and prickly with embarrassment.

And here was a message from her:

Hi Evie, I haven't seen you in ages. Would love to meet up for a coffee.

Before, I would have been grateful to receive this message. I would have pushed down my hurt for a chance to be liked again and would have arranged to meet the next day, desperately wanting to be friends.

Instead I replied: *The reason we haven't seen each other for three years is because you turned your back on me when I needed your friendship. So no, I don't want to meet with you. Evie*

I pressed send! I couldn't believe it! Being insecure had made me weak and an easy target. Not anymore. It felt so good to be strong. It felt like the greatest change that happened while we were away was me.

I was feeling good, our family trip to Sri Lanka was fully booked, and we were ready to hit the road again. Everything was working out.

CHAPTER 15

Here we go again

In January 2018, we set off on our very first family tour—a fourteen-day trip around Sri Lanka organised by Carlie and me with six families from all over the world. It was a fabulous trip, and I was so happy to share our favourite parts of Sri Lanka with them: Sigiriya, the elephants at Minneriya, sitting in the doorway of the blue train, hiking Little Adam's Peak and swimming at Hiriketiya.

The next six months were different for Emmie and me. It felt like travel had become our norm now, and it was easy and effortless. There were no fewer challenges or things that went wrong, but we'd settled into an easy groove. I knew that this was our last dash for a while, because we had to get back and get Emmie into school, more for maintaining friendships than for education, and we would need to save for another big adventure.

From Sri Lanka, we flew into Kuala Lumpur, one of our favourite cities in the world and always good for a visit. Emmie loves having the chance to do kid stuff like visiting the Sunway Lagoon theme park, KidZania and the science discovery centre, Petrosains. We loved the Petronas Towers, Batu Caves, the $3 movies and roaming around, eating street food and visiting beautiful temples and mosques. We walked to Masjid Negara, the National Mosque of Malaysia, and visited the stunning pink Putra Mosque in Putrajaya. We met many lovely people in Kuala Lumpur, including Zetty and her family, who picked us up from our hotel and showed us the places locals love in their fabulous city.

We took a bus south to Melaka and stayed for a week, riding around town in trishaws decorated with soft toys and flashing lights, and with Celine Dion songs or 'Baby Shark' blaring from speakers mounted on their bikes. Two young local women, Zati and Amalina, messaged us and offered to take us out for the day. Their generosity in sharing their town and their time with us was beautiful.

At Pulau Rawa, off Malaysia's east coast, we played in white-sand beaches and snorkelled over reefs before spending a week in the Maldives, where we swam with turtles, spotted baby stingrays and reef sharks, and walked across the whitest of white sandbars.

Our next adventure was another one of Emmie's choices. She has always loved sea glass, and is fascinated by the frosty chunks of glass flung ashore by the ocean and their beautiful tumbling past that smooths the roughest of edges. We'd scour the beaches at home in Sydney but would mostly find whites, browns and the occasional green. Emmie was obsessed with the beautiful colours that the ocean gave up in other parts of the world, so she researched online and discovered that ice blues, greens and pinks, as well as rare bonfire glass—pieces fused together by heat and embedded with ash or sand—could be found scattered over a little beach in southern Japan.

'Mummy, I've found where we should go next!' she announced, so thrilled with the little report she had written for me. 'The best place to find sea glass and bonfire glass anywhere in Asia is called Sea Glass Beach, and it's in Okinawa, Japan,' she read. 'Can we please go there?'

And so another destination had been decided, and we flew off to Tokyo. We'd been warned that Japan was expensive, so we tried to spend as little as we could, exploring on foot and visiting temples, parks and gardens. We loved the budget food at 7–11, where we could find almost anything to eat and it was all fresh, cheap and delicious. We gobbled octopus salads, onigiri, edamame and fried chicken. The supermarket near our apartment even had its own public eating area where people could heat up their store-bought meals in a microwave—such a simple but brilliant idea! So we saved our pennies any way that we could and then used them to have the experiences that cost a little more.

We mastered the train system and were amazed at how organised everything was, from the exquisite punctuality of the intimidatingly stylish office workers to the swift greetings and service given at coffee shops and stores. We often saw young people bowing and paying respect to their seniors in public, and it was so impressive. Surprisingly for someone who runs from routine and organisation, I was obsessed with Tokyo's polished efficiency—it felt like I could easily automate my life here—and Emmie just loved it.

'Mum, I can live here, if you want us to,' she said, giving Tokyo the Emmie Seal of Approval. *Maybe, Emmie. Maybe.*

We visited the beautiful Meiji Shrine at sunset, cheered for our favourites in a huge arena at a sumo wrestling match, ate rainbow cheese toast, fairy floss, animal-shaped ice-creams and colourful cookie sandwiches in Harajuku and walked to the best outdoor playground we've ever seen at Heiwa-no-Mori Park. We posed in photo booths with music blaring, and our faces were automatically altered to have larger eyes, clearer skin and pinker lips. We stumbled across rockabillies dancing at Yoyogi Park, crossed the famous Shibuya Crossing, had lunch at the Monster Cafe, and went to the top of Tokyo Tower, where we looked out over the city. We didn't stop, as there was always something to see and do.

Of course, we visited Disneyland and DisneySea for a day each, and loved the Japanese dedication to dressing up in character and kawaii outfits. We were stuck on the Star Tours ride for a while after it stopped due to a small tremor, which is apparently very normal in Tokyo. It unnerved me, but the people on the ride kindly reassured us that everything would be fine while we waited for the ride to restart. Our first earthquake.

Each day at 5.00 pm, soft music was played over a loudspeaker system and floated throughout the city; we could hear it wherever we were. I discovered that it was a daily test of the emergency alert network and a signal for children to go home for dinner. These sweet little moments were everywhere.

When we flew south to the tropics and Okinawa, we were ready for the beach and a slower pace. Due to Emmie's great success on the arcade games in Akihabara, we now had a massive hedgehog, a chipmunk and three smaller stuffed toys along with us. I ended up carrying them most of the time, of course. I would just shake my head and wonder how I let this happen.

Hannah was a friend from Instagram, and this lovely woman and her two daughters collected Emmie and me from Okinawa Airport, gave us a tour of Naha city and dropped us at our hotel. We loved spending time with them over the next few days, wandering the streets of Naha, exploring the Mihama American Village, shooting down the Okinawa roller slides, eating the famous Blue Seal ice-cream and visiting their home on the marine base.

Okinawa was much lazier for us than Tokyo, even though there was just as much to do. We watched a Ryukyuan dance performance in the streets, made artworks using traditional coral pattern-making and explored the ancient Shuri Castle. We hired a car and drove around the island, taking our time and stopping for swims wearing felt-soled boots we'd bought at an army supply store. Unexpectedly, we'd discovered a bit of danger in the oceans around Okinawa, especially the deadly stonefish, cone shells and scorpion fish. We trod carefully, and marine dangers or not, we loved this gentle pace of life.

Finally, we arrived at Sea Glass Beach, driving through farmland along a sandy road to the edge of the beach as the sun was setting. Emmie jumped out of the car and raced down to the sand, where she immediately found a beautiful piece of blue and black bonfire glass.

'Look, Mummy, look!' she screamed, running up to show me.

We walked along the tidemark, spotting flat round stones, shells and smooth pieces blue, green and white glass. A group of young American soldiers from the nearby base was also beachcombing and said hello, offering Emmie some of their prizes. It was getting late, so we left for our guesthouse, returning early the next day with our cossies and snorkels, and a bucket for the glass we planned to collect. We spent the day swimming and collecting, although I did more of it than Emmie, always searching for the next amazing piece. At the end of the day, we wandered home, tired and content. We finished our loop of the island a little worse for wear after I backed the car into a tree, but we were still in high spirits. Even when charging you for damaging their vehicles, the Japanese are sweet, polite and friendly.

I'd had no idea that Japan was so tropical. The southern islands are Maldives-level beautiful, with such stunning beaches that we had to explore more. We flew further south to Ishigaki-jima, an island in the Yaeyama chain, and based ourselves there while we explored the island in another hire car, which survived our jaunt unscathed.

We've always taken a somewhat random approach to how we travel, and driving around this island was no different. There were certain places we wanted to see, like Kabira Beach, the Uganzaki Lighthouse and Shisa Park—an outdoor sculpture gallery of huge shisas (part-dog, part-lion statues from Okinawan folklore that ward off evil spirits)—but we always left time to just look around. So when we took a series of random turns and ended up on a very narrow one-way dirt road, finally popping out at an old, overgrown picnic ground, we decided to explore.

'Let's have a look around, shall we Emmie? At least stretch our legs?'

We walked past concrete chairs and tables, unused and covered in climbing grass, and found a small creek. While we were dipping our toes in, we heard children laughing upstream.

'What do you reckon, should we go check it out?' I asked.

'Yep, Mum, let's do it,' said Emmie. We returned to the car to put our cossies on and then waded towards the laughter along the stony riverbank.

After a few minutes, we arrived at a hidden waterhole surrounded by lush green foliage where three children were swimming as their dad looked on. They were taking turns swinging from a rope swing and jumping from the top of a huge rock, and Emmie sat and watched them, itching to have a turn.

'Do you think they would let me play with them?' she whispered.

'Of course, darling, off you go,' I said. She jumped in and swam over to the kids, and they showed her how to climb the rocks and swing into the pool. Unexpected and unplanned always came through with the best goods.

At the beautiful Kabira Beach, we were hosted by Club Med, spending five days with the kind and fun Korean, Taiwanese and Japanese guests, snorkelling, swimming and learning to stand-up paddleboard and windsurf. It was blissful and easy. Staying at an all-inclusive resort was a new experience for us, and I was interested to see if we would like it. We loved it.

One of the things I struggled with while travelling, and I think all mums do but especially solo mums, is that mums have to *be* the entertainment on holidays. We're on the slides, we're making up the games, we're playing the games, our on-switch is flicked all the time, and it's pretty exhausting. At Club Med, I discovered that it doesn't have to be that way. Everything was included and organised, and the entertainment was provided so all we had to do was join in. Emmie and I had so much fun doing aqua aerobics, playing pool games and swimming together with no pressure on me to coordinate anything. It also gave Emmie a little more independence, as she was able to check herself in and out of the Mini Club. After breakfast each morning, she would run off to sign in and do trapeze, tightrope-walking and other fun activities, and then meet me at the pool. In the afternoons we snorkelled, learned how to windsurf and went stand-up paddleboarding and kayaking across the clear blue water. It was so much fun and opened my eyes to a way of holidaying that I hadn't been aware of before. It was the perfect complement to our unplanned, budget travel.

We left Club Med and moved to a small hotel in Ishigaki town, the jumping-off point for visiting many other islands around the chain. The ferry terminal was close by, and we would wander down and choose where we'd go for the day, buy a ticket and jump onto the next boat. Our first trip was to Taketomi-jima, and we rode around the sandy streets on bikes, took a ride in a traditional ox cart and waded into clear blue water from white-sand beaches. On Iriomote-jima, we kayaked through the national park, climbed up to a waterfall and swam in rock pools all afternoon. It was so much more than I ever expected to find in Japan and again opened my eyes to exploring beyond our expectations. You can never see enough, and there are so many surprises out in the world that are far beyond what we know.

Just before we left Okinawa, Emmie's tooth fell out. Altogether, she had now lost six teeth while we were travelling, and while the tooth fairy came for some, in Vietnam we'd adopted the local practice and had thrown her tooth on the roof or the road. The custom is that a bottom tooth is thrown on the roof to encourage the new tooth to grow in upwards, and a top tooth should be thrown on the road, so the new tooth will grow down.

For some reason, we decided to keep this Okinawa tooth. I honestly don't know why, but I packed it into my drone bag, not knowing that we were tempting fate.

A few days later, my bank card stopped working. I found out it had been hacked from Indonesia and money was stolen, so the bank had cancelled it. Then Emmie lost her favourite little purse. My other card didn't work in Japan, so we had no access to our money. I had to use my sister's credit card to pay for our accommodation in Ishigaki, and the super-nice front-desk person let me take money out using her card number, too. Thank goodness there were kind people who came to our rescue all through our travels. We had been lucky until now, but more inconveniences and annoying mishaps kept us on our toes. Something wasn't right; we were off-balance.

We returned to Vietnam for a few weeks to catch up with friends and get some spirit-town goodness in Hội An. I had forgotten that the tooth was in my drone bag and, as we were leaving Danang Airport, we were asked to put our big pack through a final scanner. Even though I wasn't asked to, I put my daypack on the belt, too, and the woman looked at me apologetically.

'You have a drone,' she said. 'You cannot bring it into Vietnam from this airport.'

Oh no, my drone was being confiscated! We were taken to a little room, where I filled out a form with all my details and was told to retrieve the drone on our way out of the country. We were so lucky that we were leaving from the same airport, and so there my drone stayed. In a way, I was kind of relieved … I didn't feel any pressure to take drone pics for the entire time I was in Hội An!

In Hội An, we were telling a Vietnamese friend about Emmie's tooth and how we had kept it.

'Why did you keep the tooth?' Nii Nii asked in shock. 'Keeping the tooth is very, very bad luck! You should not keep the tooth. You will have many bad things happen.'

That explained it. All the bad luck was from the bloody tooth. Well, that was simple, we would throw it on the roof. But we couldn't throw it on the roof because it was in the drone case at Danang Airport! Apparently, the bad luck would leave us alone while the tooth wasn't in our possession, but as soon as we had the drone case back we would have to get the tooth out and get rid of it!

After two weeks of friends, pho and fun, we left Hội An and retrieved the drone from security at Danang Airport. We grabbed the tooth out of the bag, and Emmie took a huge run-up and threw it on top of a bus shed just outside the departures hall. Mission accomplished, we set off for Bali for a few weeks. Bad luck begone!

We arrived late at night and took a taxi straight to our guesthouse in Sanur. The next day, I couldn't find my daypack, with my Sony camera, GoPro and drone inside it.

'Um, Emmie, have you seen my daypack?' I asked as I looked around the room, confused that I couldn't see it. We searched everywhere and couldn't find it. I spoke to the villa manager, and I called the driver who had picked us up from the airport. I looked at our photos, and I couldn't spot it anywhere.

'Mum,' Emmie said seriously, 'this is a shambles. I reckon you've left the bag at the airport.'

Of course I had. Sometimes my brain just can't manage everything, especially arriving late with the bags and Emmie and her menagerie of stuffed toys. Something had been left behind, and unfortunately it wasn't a stuffed bloody hedgehog—it was my bag of camera gear.

We had to go back, but the airport was shut because the Mount Agung volcano was erupting and all flights had been cancelled.

'Well, let's just go to the airport and see if we can get in,' I said with a shrug. We called a car, and off we went.

Ngurah Rai International Airport was deserted. It was eerie to be in a place that was usually bustling and chaotic, and filled with tourists coming and going. There was no one around except a few security guards lingering outside. Luckily, though, the arrivals doors were open. We sneaked in, past immigration and customs, and wandered the deserted arrival halls trying to figure out what to do next. We found a guard inside, and he sent us off to a few different places to check for the bag, and while everywhere was a dead-end in our search for the cameras, we weren't giving up.

'How do you feel, Emmie? Are we getting the bag back?' I asked her when it seemed like we didn't have any more options.

'Yes, I still think it's coming back,' she said. 'I can feel it in my witchy bones.'

'Yeah, me too!' I was a little anxious, but I felt optimistic that we were going to find it. 'Let's just keep trying.' We stayed calm and just kept asking staff if there was anything else we could do.

A young guard we were talking to told us to wait while he called the security team on his walkie-talkie. It must have been a pretty boring day at work for him with the airport closed, and we were super lucky that we had him and the airport all to ourselves. He asked me what flight we were on, what time we arrived, and what we were wearing. In the office, on the other end of the line, security staff dug out the footage from when we arrived, and they tracked me via CCTV. They saw me get our bags off the belt and load them onto a trolley, walk out of arrivals, meet our driver and walk over to the carpark. They saw us load the car with all the bags except my daypack, which was left on the ground at the pick-up area.

'We have your bag,' the guard said. 'You left it in the carpark, and it is with security in the domestic terminal.'

OMG, no way! We had been staying hopeful and optimistic, but I couldn't believe that the bag with thousands of dollars worth of camera equipment was coming back! Mostly I couldn't believe that we'd left it in the carpark … but how amazing that security had it. Emmie gave the guard a big hug and off we went to the security office at the domestic terminal.

'There are always good people in the world, Emmie, aren't there? We are so lucky.'

'Well, Mum, it's because we threw that tooth away. It was stealing our luck, and now we have it back. High-five, woman!'

Yay, hooray, our luck was back. We found the security office and collected our bag from the Balinese officers with all our valuable equipment inside. Amazing. Thank you so much to the Ngurah Rai International Airport security team! We love you.

⌣

A few days later, I got an email from the real estate agent who was managing our home while we were away.

'The tenants want to break the lease early,' she said. 'They'll move out in two months. Please let me know if you want to advertise it again and get new tenants in.'

This was a sign. It was time to go home.

I told Emmie about the email. 'Are you ready to go home for a bit, Emmie?'

'Mum, if we can move back into our own home, then I am happy to go back,' she said. And it was agreed. It was time to try to make our way back to the real world, for a while at least. It was time to rest and to settle in for a bit. I didn't have any fears going back this time, and we still had two months before we would head home, so it wasn't like we were going back straight away. I felt okay with it, though.

I wasn't sure that I was going to like it. But I wasn't scared.

My sister had just arrived in Phnom Penh, Cambodia, to start a job with Friends-International, a global social enterprise that helps children and families break the poverty cycle. Her role was with its ChildSafe Movement, a program that empowers everyone, from tourists to businesses and tuk-tuk drivers, to protect children from harm. We were going to leave Bali and meet her there in a week when she had settled in. She called me on her second day, telling me that she felt really sick and had a bad pain in her belly.

'Oh, maybe you just need to go and do a poo,' I laughed, the uncaring sister. 'I'm sure it's nothing.'

Within 24 hours, she was being evacuated to Bangkok for an emergency appendectomy. Mum was beside herself and decided to fly over to Phnom Penh, too, and when Ren returned from Bangkok Hospital, we all rocked up on her doorstep.

Our time in Phnom Penh was different to the year before. We got to know it a little better, and while the poverty was often overwhelming, this time I got into its heart. We spent time exploring and met families living in temple grounds and under tarpaulins next to railway tracks. We bought bags of rice for these families, and we gave food to kids we saw collecting rubbish on the street. It's a tough balance, and while I'd always known to

273

never give money to people and to help with food instead, if I ever saw those children again, I'd want to give them everything I had.

This is where my sister's work is so valuable. The ChildSafe Movement has a hotline for locals and tourists to call when they see at-risk children, and social workers spring into action to help them and their families. The Khmer people need our help, but it has to be done the right way.

We discovered Cambodian architect Van Molyvann's legacy on this visit, too, exploring the Phnom Penh Olympic Stadium and University on a brilliant architecture tour and learning more about how advanced society was here before the Khmer Rouge. We went on a street-food tour that started at a rooftop bar and ended with us all fighting for the toilet a few hours later. It was pretty dire. Mum ended up at the medical centre on a drip, where they filled her up with bags and bags of saline, while Emmie, Ren and I rolled around the apartment with stomach cramps.

Emmie and I travelled south to the seaside town of Kep and traipsed around crumbling 1960s beachside villas, once homes of the rich and famous, now abandoned and overgrown, symbols of the Khmer Rouge's destruction. We ate freshly caught crab at the markets, visited a Kampot pepper farm and trekked around in the rain. On our way back to Phnom Penh, we sat in the doorway of the train, arms around each other, and whispered our favourite parts of our adventure as the sun set gold and rusty over green fields and palm trees.

We hadn't been quite ready to go home to Sydney a year earlier, but now we were. Our home was waiting, and it was time.

'Okay, Emmie,' I said. 'Let's go home. But just for a while.'

CHAPTER 16

A lovely zigzag

'You chose love.'

The sharp flashes of clarity that made me trust myself and acknowledge the richness of our adventure together had come from the most unlikely places: camping on the Great Wall of China, sailing across the Bohol Sea with Emmie's head resting against my shoulder, kindness from local families, flying through the air on ziplines and sitting on a train with a stranger.

I'd been wrapped up in the rhythm and my own reminiscing when, from across the aisle, the lady spoke to me. She said she was a healer, that she had been watching us and wanted to tell me something. Her face was tanned and wrinkled, and gold bangles jingled on her arms as she reached towards me and pushed her face into mine.

'You chose love,' she whispered. 'I know these things, I can feel it,' she said as she tapped her heart with a sun-scorched hand. 'You could have chosen money, you could have chosen your career, you could have chosen things. But you didn't. You chose love.'

I looked down at Emmie sitting next to me as the fields and mountains whizzed by to the soothing beat of the wheels on the tracks. She was singing a song to herself and swinging her legs as she gazed out at the world beyond the carriage. She was confident and happy, and we were where we needed to be.

The two of us, on the road together. The dream that came true.

All throughout our journey, she had bounded from one experience to the next, trusting me to make our path and often bravely leading the way. I couldn't have asked for a better travel buddy.

The healer had been right: I did choose love.

When we left Australia on our adventure, some said that I was running away. They had it half right: I was running, but it was towards the best life I could have with Emmie. In fact, it was a sprint.

You just never know how much time you have left.

⌣

Emmie and I flew back to Sydney with Qantas, book-ending our adventure with our Aussie flying kangaroo and scoffing Tim Tams from the plane's galley while everyone slept. We soared over the Cronulla peninsula and our home near the bay before touching down early in the morning. We were back, but there was no fanfare in my heart. It was a cautious greeting without long-term commitment. I was prepared to put down roots, but they would be shallow ones. I wasn't keen on staying around too long.

The Uber dropped us off at the footpath out the front of our house. Just another fare. Just another homecoming. Just another adventure ending.

I stared at the old redbrick house. My anchor, my old path, my place in the 'burbs.

Emmie was excited. 'Our house! Our home!' she yelled as we entered, running from room to room. 'It's just like I remember it!'

The removalist arrived with the few things we'd kept, and I unpacked the suitcase of sheets, towels and pillowcases that I'd bought in Phnom Penh and had laundered before we left. I made the beds and sat in turmoil, my insides shaking. What had I done?

It's bewildering to spend so much time away and then come back to what was. Walking into our house was like travelling back in time. Did our adventure really exist? Where did those two and a half years go? How could our trip seem to last forever and then suddenly be over?

But there was no time to figure it out. The fog of routine and organisation rolled in, and I started sorting out our life. The power, the water and the wifi were reconnected. Rates and insurance were paid, and the mortgage and my mind were reset. I signed Emmie back into gymnastics and bought her uniforms and school supplies. As if pulled by a magnet, I was drawn back between the lines. With every reconnection into routine, we moved further from our whim-led life.

I had enough money to keep us ahead with the mortgage, but only just. I sold the caravan to put a little more in the bank while I tried to earn an income working from home. I wanted to be around to help Emmie adjust back into school.

At first, I re-enrolled her into the school where she had completed kindergarten. It was a tough transition. Some of the friendships she'd had before we left had changed, although, as with mine, the good ones were just as good as they were before, and friends such as Amber and Layla welcomed her home with hugs and love.

But it didn't feel right to me. I realised that I'd only enrolled Emmie in kindergarten here because I'd thought sending her to a fee-paying school showed people that I didn't fit the negative solo-mum stereotype. Now, I didn't care what people thought, so I changed her to the local public school, where she began to thrive in its kind and supportive environment.

Dealing with Emmie's father was no different to before, but this time around I was less scared, spent less time worrying and stood up more for myself and us. Emmie is a pretty smart kid and accepts him for who he is.

'Everyone loves differently,' I tell her.

Coming home wasn't easy, but it wasn't as tough as I thought it would be. I had days when I felt sad and disconnected, and questioned what I was doing here, but I told myself that was normal. And I didn't want to feel settled anyway; knowing this life isn't for me long-term keeps me on my toes, always searching for new adventures and planning another big trip.

Being back felt different—*I* felt different. I'd let myself go in all the ways that used to give me confidence—I weighed more, I was less groomed, I had only basic clothes—and yet I felt better about myself than I ever had. Where before I had criticised myself, now I accepted myself—and that in itself was life-changing.

I wish I'd loved myself for all those years. It makes me sad to look back and see that for so long I didn't believe in me, that I doubted myself, questioned myself and hated my body.

I had to break away to discover this, to know the power of loving myself and how easy it is to do it once you really try. Believing in myself is the greatest power I have. I know who I am and where my heart is. And these feelings flow onto Emmie, too; as she sees me happy and strong and confident, she grows more in that direction, too.

There are still days when a snake uncoils in my belly, when I wake up and wonder what I am doing back here. I mourn our days on the road, but for this year, our life is in one place.

Now that we've been back for a few months, I've realised that I love our little home as it is, and I've stopped trying to improve it for others. We don't have very much, spending what I make on bills and living, and putting the little that's left towards travel. I'm happy with that. It's different to how we lived before we left: we have much less money but more love and togetherness.

I'd choose this every time.

Emmie was blessed to have been able to spend so much time travelling, and I honestly believe kids who travel will change the world. It opens their eyes and their minds, and teaches them resilience, confidence and acceptance of people, culture and religions that are different to what they know from home. And right now the world needs acceptance more than ever before.

Travel showed Emmie that while the world is big, it's not scary. Wherever we went, she could find a friendly face and make a connection, even though these friends might not look like her or speak the same language. It showed her the fragility of our environment as we hiked and sailed and explored. She learned about history, architecture, religion, ancient tribes and wildlife. She ran barefoot through back streets and made friends with kids everywhere we went. And, most importantly, she got to spend time with me. We lived our life together, and often we were lucky enough to be with local families or other travelling families, and we learned about them, too.

Back home, community has been our key to settling in. Recently, Emmie sold hydrangeas from our garden in a little stall out the front of our house. I ran back and forth, cutting flowers from the beautiful old tree in our backyard and taking her little bunches. We met our neighbours, who wandered down and bought posies. They were so generous with their encouragement of Emmie, and I felt myself softening, just a little. A sense of belonging started to return.

Emmie also started Nippers down at the beach on Sunday mornings. My stubborn little girl, who has a habit of giving up if she doesn't master a skill immediately, showed huge heart in swimming and board paddling, trying her best and persevering. At a carnival the day after our hydrangea sale, she entered the board race. She was knocked off over and over again by the waves but, to my surprise and joy, she kept getting back on. She was still paddling hard, way out past the breakers, when the other girls had finished.

She came in last by about five minutes, and as she ran up the sand to the finish line, the kids and parents on the beach clapped and cheered her on. My happiness gave me tears. I was so proud of my baby for not giving up, and I realised that, while for a long time I couldn't see it, there was kindness around me here at home, too.

⌣

Some people seem to have everything figured out. And maybe through the social media lens, I seem that way, too. I hope not, because I don't.

I'm an average mum who had a big dream. I just made that dream come true.

Whatever your dream is, you have to give it a shot. Dare to make your magic happen. There will never be a perfect time. There's just now.

And don't listen to the negative, cautious what-ifs, because what if chasing your dream is the best thing you ever do?

As I say to Emmie, you were made by a one-in-a-million sperm that made it to the egg. You've already beaten the odds. You're already a champion. How will you make your life even more amazing?

Sometimes the biggest challenge is believing in yourself, and taking control of your own life. It took me a long time to realise that I don't have to follow the path I was encouraged to, that my life was mine to create and shape to my will and my dreams.

We are born into this incredible world of mountains, jungles, oceans, islands, waterfalls and wildlife, and yet so many of us live in concrete, in dense suburbs, in deadlines and debt, working and worrying about when we will have enough, when we will be enough, and always wanting more. We chase a life that we think will make us happy, that will be easier and more rewarding. But we don't need to chase it, because it's right here! It's been here all the time. This beautiful, magical world is all around us, just waiting for us to step outside, to take a chance and explore it all.

The future for Emmie and me will always have travel in it. I will never stop. Emmie will never stop.

'I want to travel full-time again soon,' I said to Emmie the other day.

'Me, too!' Emmie said. 'Why do you want to?'

'Because I love it.'

'Who doesn't?' she replied. 'Let's go travelling again. And then stay put. Travel, stay put, travel, stay put. Our life, the zigzag.'

A lovely zigzag. From backyard to backpack and back again.

Two peas on an aeroplane

by Emmie Farrell

Once upon time there was a Mama Pea and a Baby Pea. Mama Pea went to work in the city every day, while Baby Pea had a babysitter. Mama Pea didn't get to see Baby Pea that much because whenever Mama Pea got home from work, Baby Pea was already asleep.

Mama Pea was sad and wanted to have more time with Baby Pea, so she decided that she would spend all her savings to go travelling with Baby Pea. Mama Pea and Baby Pea travelled all around the world, mostly in Asia, and they had a wonderful time.

Mama Pea and Baby Pea grew closer and closer. Then, after more than two years, they came back to their pea pod in Australia. They put all their old furniture in, and Baby Pea even got her own pea-pod treehouse!

They restarted their lives back in their pod after their life-changing journey. Mama Pea now works at home, and Baby Pea can see her all the time, except when Baby Pea is at school.

They are happy, but they are always happiest when they are setting off on an adventure and are two peas on an aeroplane.

Thank you

Emmie and I set off travelling so we could spend time together. We never felt alone, because we had each other and we had amazing support and love from so many people at home and around the world. Thank you so much to our family and friends from home, the local families and travelling families we met on the road and the wonderful friends we made through social media, all of whom gave us advice, support, information and help along the way. Every little message and comment meant so much to us.

A few people had said that I should write a book about our trip, and my friend Bryce Corbett got me started writing a few chapters. About a year later, Jane Morrow from Murdoch Books saw a Q&A I did in *The Squiz* (coincidentally organised by Bryce) and emailed me: *Have you thought about writing a book?* Emmie and I were at my sister's apartment in Phnom Penh with my mum, and I still remember it so clearly. I had this feeling of fearful excitement, and also felt very privileged that Jane thought our story was worthy of sharing.

We were on our way home after two and a half years on the road, and so even though our travels paused, a new journey started: writing this very book. It was infinitely more difficult than travelling the world with Emmie, but such an insightful experience to relive our adventure and poke into what it gave us and how it changed us. I spent a lot of time reminiscing about our journey, and writing about it built another layer of love in my heart for it.

THANK YOU

Thanks to Jane and everyone at Murdoch Books for believing in our story and helping us share it.

Thank you to my mum and dad, Lyn and Ian, and my sister Ren for all their support and for allowing me to take their granddaughter and niece off on a big adventure without ever questioning my decision. To Jacqui, for always lifting me up and having a flute of bubbles waiting for me; and to Peta, Kellie, Jo and the Maggios, for their words of encouragement and love all through our trip. To Alison, for always checking in on us, and Anna, for taking the car and looking after her so well. To all the wonderful people we met along the way and who supported us: you are part of our adventure and our memories.

During the tough times before we left to travel, I had a lot of people around who helped me: Kate, who kindly forced me to go to mothers' group, Lee, Helena, Kimberly and all my mothers' group friends. Thank you to Jenny, Kim, Lesa, Julie, Carie and so many other friends from school who popped up and re-entered my life when I truly needed it. Thanks to Carlie for helping make my dream of running solo mum trips come true.

Thank you to Sophie Haslett, who first wrote about our story and helped us share our journey. Thank you to Narelle, Amelia, Mandy, Aleney, Amber, Shay, Karen and all our wonderful, supportive, thoughtful friends on Instagram and Facebook who have helped us along the way, stuck up for us online and been part of our beautiful sparkling web.

Lots of love,

289

Resources

ChildSafe Movement
A global movement empowering people to protect children.
www.thinkchildsafe.org

The Elephant Valley Project
Cambodia's ethical elephant sanctuary, where elephants roam free.
www.elephantvalleyproject.org

Friends-International
This leading social enterprise saves lives and builds the futures of the most marginalised children and youth and their families across the world.
www.friends-international.org

Mumpack Travel Club
Join the 'Mumpack Travel' club on Facebook to see upcoming Mumpack Travel trips.
www.facebook.com/MumpackTravel

Our Tribe Travels
Find everything you need to know about family travel from this amazing online community.
www.facebook.com/OurTribeTravels

Take 3 for the Sea

*An organisation that encourages you to take three pieces of
rubbish with you when you leave the beach, waterway or
anywhere, and make a difference.*
www.take3.org

Trash Hero World

Find local beach clean-ups while travelling in Asia.
www.trashhero.org or www.facebook.com/trashheroworld

Find us!

Please visit us at www.mumpacktravel.com or
@mumpacktravel on Instagram and Facebook.